Real photo postcard of coal miners taking a break in a Russell County, Virginia, coal mine, 1926. The man in the center is Frank Kilgore, "Papaw" of this book's author.

Author's Tribute: Papaw Kilgore worked forty-three years hand-drilling, hand-loading, and hand-pushing thousands of tons of coal out of a very dark and dangerous environment, day in and day out. He lost many friends and members of his extended family along the way. Many miners died or were permanently mangled, mostly in a violent and sudden fashion. Their fellow miners attended the funerals, helped the survivors best they could, and went right back into the mines. PTSD was not known then but it took its toll nonetheless.

The coal that Papaw produced (and hundreds of thousands of miners like him) helped fuel local and nationwide businesses and the rest was shipped around the globe. Millions of Americans burned coal to keep warm, heat bath water, and cook. At that time (mid-1800s to mid-1900s) in the USA, and most other countries, the mining of various minerals was the world's most dangerous occupation. All that Papaw knew was that he was feeding his family and, in a small way, assisting the rapid growth of his country and other, hopefully friendly, nations. He was humble, quiet, kind-hearted, and never started a ruckus.

My hero never drove a car. He walked a six-mile round trip each day (except most Sundays) to and from the mines, sometimes "doubling back" another shift because Appalachian coal was in such demand. He supported his family of nine in a three-room, coal-heated house. Along with his passel of kids, he raised corn, cows, hogs, and work horses on very steep hillsides, and tended a big vegetable garden on what was considered "flat plots" in those days.

Papaw died a gasping death from pneumoconiosis, a fancy name for black lung disease. He was actually luckier than most miners; when he retired he could still walk without slumping or hobbling, despite suffering many joint-related mining accidents. Toward the end, he "piddled around the house" best he could. I loved him and he loved me, despite my rowdy ways.

Coal miners do America's dirty work. They and their predecessors deserve America's respect.

The History and Culture of Coalfields Southwest Virginia
Author: Frank Kilgore
Editor: Proal Heartwell

Cover photos: Integrated crew of coalfield Virginia timber and sawmill workers near Pocahontas in 1883. UMWA coal miners and supporters during the 1989 strike in Southwest Virginia, courtesy of Earl Dotter.

Copyright 2024 by Frank Kilgore

All rights reserved.

Published by Coalfields Publishing
www.CoalfieldsPublishing.com

Book and cover design copyright © 2024 by Coalfields Publishing

ISBN-13: 978-1-7333644-6-1
Large Print ISBN-13: 978-1-7333644-7-8
Hardcover ISBN-13: 978-1-7333644-8-5

No part of this book may be reproduced in any manner without permission from the publisher, except in the case of brief quotations in reviews or articles. Information may be obtained from the publisher.

Merchants and non-profit groups wishing to sell this book may qualify for discounted pricing. Also, if a reader finds a grammatical error or documented factual mistake, please feel free to email info@CoalfieldsPublishing.com.

To my children, Joyce and Jason, no matter what few hard assets I have gained after decades of hard work, none of it would be worthwhile without the joy and challenges of fatherhood.

You all make my heart sing. Love you.

This book is also dedicated to all people who have struggled to achieve the American Dream and came from far away with nothing but hope and a willingness to work hard. Most of our forefathers and mothers would today be classified as underdogs, and that is how the United States of America came to be. Unfortunately, many of our ancestors, while seeking a better life, also created underdogs along that journey. Many humans were slaughtered to make way for expansion, or were enslaved to make life easier for the more affluent.

That is our country's history and literally the history of the human race as we all evolve and learn, sometimes painfully learning the same lessons over and over again. Hate is easy. Being objective and empathetic is apparently very difficult.

THE HISTORY AND CULTURE OF COALFIELDS SOUTHWEST VIRGINIA

FRANK KILGORE

Edited by
PROAL HEARTWELL

COALFIELDS PUBLISHING

CONTENTS

Acknowledgments — xi

PART I
THE REAL CULTURE OF SOUTHWEST VIRGINIA

1. Be Proud of Your Homeland, Far Southwest Virginia — 3
2. Think Twice Before Calling (All) Coalfield Appalachians Racists, Sexists, and Ignoramuses — 8
3. We're More Multi-Racial Than You May Think! — 17
4. The Leadership Roles of Women in Our Coalfields and the Mountain Leaders Who Supported Them — 33
5. Education and Athletics — 47
6. Our Young People Are Smart and Competitive, So Where Are the Good Jobs? — 61
7. Coalfield Virginia's Military Participation and Standouts — 67
8. Coal Mining — 79
9. The United Mine Workers of America — 85

PART II
THE NATURAL AND SOCIAL HISTORY OF FAR SOUTHWEST VIRGINIA

10. Truly, the Very Beginning of the Appalachian Coalfields — 113
11. The Ice Age in Coalfield Appalachia — 122
12. The Petra Project — 142
13. Native Americans — 153
14. Moore's Fort in Castle's Woods circa 1774 — 170
15. The Revolutionary War in the Mountains — 183
16. The History Channel Insults All Appalachians and Their Ancestors — 193
17. The Frontier Dreams of Francois Pierre De Tubeuf — 196

PART III
SOUTHWEST VIRGINIA STORIES WORTH READING

18. A Civil War Story Worth the Telling of It: The Long Way Home — 209
19. Special Feature: Two Mountain Boys Go to War — 222
20. Giving President Jimmy Carter a Jar of Honey from Honey Branch — 228

About the Author — 243
Also by Frank Kilgore — 245

ACKNOWLEDGMENTS

Thanks to all my friends and family members that reviewed the many, many drafts of this book, or claimed to do so. A special shout-out to Proal Heartwell, a Charlottesville native who came to our mountains in the late 1970s to help implement the federal surface mining laws that guard our mountains and coalfield residents from abuse and neglect. He is the co-founder of the Village School for Girls (and tomorrow's leaders) grades 5-8. His edits were precise, plentiful, and very much appreciated. It would take another book to quote Proal's Banacek truisms that I naively try to live by. One in particular baffled me until a late-night epiphany: "When an owl comes to a mouse picnic, he is not there for the sack race." That's Socrates stuff.

Proal Heartwell

Clinch Valley College, now The University of Virginia's College at Wise (UVAW), has since the mid-1950s provided Appalachian students with an affordable opportunity to gain a post-high school education; an education that would have otherwise been very difficult or literally impossible to achieve. Thousands of Appalachians, young and old, have gained knowledge and specific skills from this reputable institution. For example, many, many teachers from our mountains got their degree at UVAW and share, or have shared, their craft in Central Appalachia's public schools. Although paid less than the state and national averages, these dedicated educators pass on the torch of knowledge to each succeeding generation in a nurturing fashion.

The college started as a two-year program in 1954, eventually gained full undergraduate credentials, and has, over the years, established a smidgen of master degree programs that hopefully will be expanded. At some point, sooner than later please, the school's mothership, the University of Virginia, will invest some of its wealth and prestige toward UVAW by supporting much-needed doctorate programs that will advance even more Appalachian students toward crucial and high-paying careers.

As UVAW graduates choose to stay in our coal communities to do good, or return home after they find out that life in a slower lane can be very rewarding, the better off our region will be. Speaking of graduate schools, UVAW's students have a consistent reputation for being the most-prepped graduate school candidates from the five-state mountain region. That did not happen by accident.

And a special thanks to the professors and leaders I met and learned from at then Clinch Valley College. **Professor Helen Lewis**, a strong Appalachian woman from northern Georgia, inspired many students to actively push quality-of-life improvements in the coalfields at a time when "ladies" were mostly seen but not heard. Thankfully the Helens of the world were successful in passing forward long-awaited opportunities to their successors.

Dr. Lewis: Clinch Valley College annual, mid-1950s

Helen in a Welsh coal mine. Miners from Wales visited Clinch Valley College and our Virginia coalfields in the mid-1970s due to her interest in comparable studies.

UVAW grads should also learn about and tip their hats to **Chancellor Joe Smiddy**, Clinch Valley College's most successful leader, who worked incredibly hard for decades to make this "college-on-a-hill" dream come true. Without him, and the local leaders that came up with this monumental idea, I and a huge number of other working-class students would not have what we have and can share today. Thanks to higher education, whether academic or trade skills, coalfield Appalachia is transitioning its static economy to one of variety and options previously unavailable.

UVAW charter chancellor, Joe Smiddy, taking a break from playing mountain music which he liberally shared with everyone.

Last, but not least, past and current state legislators made sure the state of Virginia never forgot our mountain mission of a school. Special thanks particularly go to former state senator **William Wampler, Jr.** and veteran house member **Terry Kilgore** (a Clinch Valley College alumnus); the last few decades of growth are the result of their visions and legislative prowess. Many more academic leaders, state and federal legislators, benefactors, and loyal graduates are to be honored as well. There are way too many to count, thankfully.

Delegate Terry Kilgore

Newly minted state senator William Wampler, Jr., on the right, and his father, William (Bill) Wampler, Sr., who served the Fighting Ninth Southwest Virginia Congressional District seat for two decades. His constituents and the press dubbed him the "Bald Eagle" of Southwest Virginia.

Veteran Virginia Delegate Terry Kilgore, of Scott County, posing on the left with Governor Ralph Northam as they celebrate the grand opening of the Clinch River State Park near St. Paul, Virginia.

NOTE: The author owned this land, and decades ago developed a private outdoor venue that was open to the public for free. This 220-acre historical setting is now the centerpiece of the newest state park. The property was first called Saint Marie on the Clinch and was the residence of a coal baron from France who attempted a French Settlement in the 1790s that included nearly all the coal land in Southwest Virginia west of the Clinch River. Much later, the farm was known as Sugar Hill due to the production of maple syrup and sugar. The Frenchman's story is told later in this book.

PART I
THE REAL CULTURE OF SOUTHWEST VIRGINIA

CHAPTER 1
BE PROUD OF YOUR HOMELAND, FAR SOUTHWEST VIRGINIA

IN THIS BOOK YOU WILL, perhaps for the first time, learn the good things about Virginia's coalfield region and its history of cultural diversity and unique biodiversity. Those two factors found in the far southwestern corner of our beautiful Commonwealth of Virginia have not been appropriately documented and disseminated. For example, you will learn in later chapters that our ancestors turned the tide of the Revolutionary War, mined coal under extremely dangerous working conditions to power the Industrial Revolution, helped the world win two global wars, embraced women's rights and racial integration in a state (and the entire South) that rejected both not so long ago.

Thankfully our grandparents, parents, and other elders have also passed down a culture of friendliness, patriotism, and a love of independence. This Appalachian culture is worth saving and is a source of our everlasting pride. And even if you don't have mountain ancestors from here, you are welcomed to our verdant homeland to bring new energy, bring creative ideas and jobs, raise children, get involved in civic programs and leadership roles, and enjoy and extend our friendly culture. Know that your ancestors (that voluntarily came to the New World) wherever their origins also yearned for the same opportunities and freedom that our ancestors struggled to achieve. This hodgepodge of humanity is called America.

This is not to say we don't suffer from a lack of good-paying jobs and optimism. However, during the past few decades, and with the help of the Appalachian Regional Commission and state and federal legislators, our Appalachian homeland has greatly improved in the areas of infrastructure, education, health care, and the environment.

Bluntly stated, our persistent poverty levels come directly from the lack of regional generational wealth, too many harmful stereotypes, and a lack of sustained effective local leadership. Speculators from the 1880s through the 1940s bought out most of the natural resources in the coalfields from our ancestors for pennies on the dollar. Locals were either hoodwinked or simply needed quick cash without thinking of the region's future. Living off of wages generated by a mainly natural resource extraction economy always leads to job losses and severe poverty when those commodities are gone or no longer needed by the world market. With a lot of hard ongoing work, planning, and funding, our coalfields are being revitalized by tourism, conservation programs, improved education, and non-coal-related job training.

Why, you may ask, is Southwest Virginia's coalfield region a good place to live? Imagine waking up to the news that a hurricane is bearing down on your community; killer tornadoes are ravaging the landscape and people; raging forest fires are burning entire towns and communities; severe droughts are devastating economic growth, food production, and public funds; or residents are being harmed or intimidated by riots and gangs that have taken over large swaths of cities. If that kind of life is progress, coalfield Virginia is very lucky not to be part of it. But we do have plenty of Nature's bounty to make up for the lack of big city lights or whole regions tortured by repeated natural disasters.

We do have, and many times take for granted, our green mountains, lively streams and rivers, some of the most rare and endangered flora and fauna in North America, four moderate seasons, great public schools, and relatives and neighbors who care what happens to us and our families.

These tangible and intangible assets are priceless, and we have it all here in a region of Virginia that has been the butt of stereotypical insults for centuries. We used to ignore such bigotry because we knew what we had, and when economic times were good we didn't care what the outside world thought of us. Now things are changing as we march toward better jobs and opportunities that will allow our young, smart people to take on or create good-paying work that they can certainly handle if given the chance. Just as helpful, we are seeing an influx of industrious people from other parts of the nation and the world bringing new energy, new ideas, and new spending power as they voluntarily embrace our natural assets and social culture.

No longer should we be embarrassed when someone mocks our Old World accent (Appalachian dialect). That accent is our history and those bigots can be put in their place quickly, if needed. Instead of hiding or making excuses regarding our culture and roots, we should embrace them and ask the people who say otherwise what is *their* history, culture, sense of duty, and love of country and family? And what about their respect for people who fight crime, fires, and diseases? Stand your ground like other mocked cultures do and turn a new page with the knowledge that coalfield Virginia has many intangible assets our nation yearns for. Fight back. Reject the harassment, and the culture bullies will retreat. I know this for a fact. For too long we have resorted to root denial when castigated. No more.

As we demand respect we also need, in return, to respect other people not like us. Respect requires being respectful.

This book also reveals our tragedies, successes, greatness, and woes. We are not perfect by a long shot, but it's time to put up a fight; our Scots, Irish, Scots-Irish, English, Welsh, and Germanic generations have never backed away from a scuffle. Just as impoverished city dwellers must tire of being wholly characterized as drug dealers or takers, gang-bangers, and natural-born killers, so are mountain people sick and tired of being misjudged and ridiculed at will.

At least African Americans were offended enough to form the NAACP and many other unified counter-punchers. Jewish communities also have their effective anti-defamation leagues to fight bigotry so serious that their people have literally been murdered by the millions simply for existing. Migrant workers also have a sympathetic media and organized groups to push their causes on a daily basis. Yet, native coalfield Appalachians are treated with unfettered disdain. We have a lot in common with these and other distinct cultures in terms of being perpetual underdogs. Hopefully, positive change for all is in the air.

Appalachians, of course, are not the most oppressed population in our great nation by a long shot, but we sure understand that bigotry and slander are a major cause of lack of investments, good jobs, and hope. Who is going to invest in our young, smart people (many of whom would love to remain in, or come back to, their mountain homes) if all that potential investors hear is bad-mouth drivel spouted from unlearned sources? Not many.

But the investors—angel or otherwise—who do give us a shot are generally greatly rewarded with affordable labor and land, bolstered by dedicated employees. They also enjoy a friendly atmosphere and some of the most accommodating people on earth. Literally, a sizable working farm and a sense of peace can be purchased here for the price of one D.C. brownstone.

My Scots-Irish family has been in the Appalachian Mountains since 1770, and many of them fought in the Battle of King's Mountain, a turning point in the Revolutionary War according to none other than Thomas Jefferson, two more presidents, and the defeated British supreme commander. We stay here because of Nature's beauty, family, roots, and sense of home. We want our future generations to have this choice as well. Fortunately, our coalfield society is wide open to new residents if they come here for the right reasons and with open minds.

If a traveler will simply listen, the biggest difference in the various sub-regions of Appalachia is fairly easy to figure out. The further north one ventures, the more likely it is that vowels are more fully enunciated as we speak. That is pretty much the sum-total difference, regardless of race, religion, or politics.

We coalfield citizens are mostly rural, usually conservative, somewhat libertarian, accommodating to strangers, love our verdant hills and hollers, and tend to be patriotic and family-oriented to a fault. Statistics, successes and failures, and weather patterns differ from northern Alabama to the Pennsylvania/New York state line. Our overall mountain culture is widespread. And yes, just like impoverished communities around the world, we do struggle with poor health, bad choices, drugs, and chronic economic recessions.

This book is not about denial of our human faults and self-inflicted conditions; it's simply an opportunity to point out many of the good aspects of our homeland, culture, and history that go unreported by most of the media and almost every elitist. J.D. Vance, author of *Hillbilly Elegy,* is the most galling and uppity pontificator of the bunch.

The similarities between far left and far right radicals are striking. Just like many other holier-than-thou misled revolutionaries throughout history, these toxic participants hate to the nth degree the freedom of opposing thoughts and expressions. As a result, scorched-earth politicians of both major parties have manipulated extreme, cynical, divisive people for a long time, but the past couple of decades seem to have been much worse. If keyboard warriors had to reveal their real identities, I suspect online threats and vicious slander would shrink immediately. Anonymous commentators are cowards all.

The bottom line is that we Americans have the right to state our opinions as long as we do not promote violence or harm others by outright malicious slander.

CHAPTER 2
THINK TWICE BEFORE CALLING (ALL) COALFIELD APPALACHIANS RACISTS, SEXISTS, AND IGNORAMUSES

DURING PRESIDENT OBAMA's re-election bid, a radio commentator stated with certainty that the conservative "Hillbilly Firewall" would hinder his election to another term in states with sizable Appalachian districts. That prediction was not a compliment to our mountain region on many fronts, but it did indicate that the negative stereotyping of mountain residents appears to be the last politically correct bigotry promoted by many segments of the media and elite societies.

The coalfield region of the infamous Hillbilly Firewall is shown below.

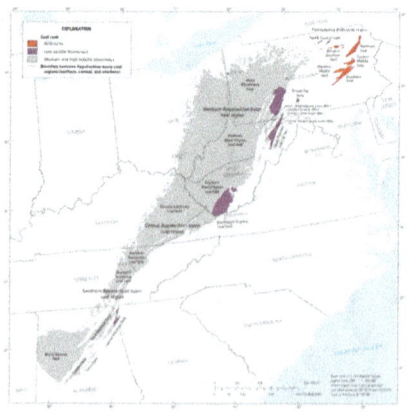

And the relatively small coalfield mining region of Virginia is depicted in this map.

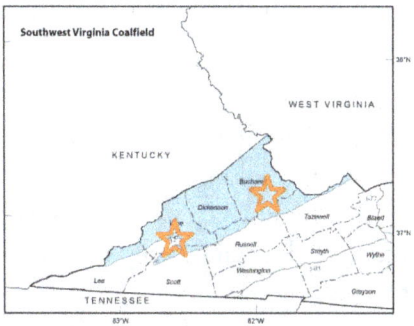

Not that facts should get in the way of news commentators' pithy slurs, but perhaps we can use the coalfields of Virginia as a potential case-in-point and counterweight to such bigotry.

For example, the small coal-mining town of Norton, Virginia, started an integrated four-team Little League program in 1951, the first such program in the entire South. Charlottesville's team won the eastern title, and its handlers demanded that the Norton's Black players be taken off the team before the state title game commenced. Norton, having the only Little League program in western Virginia, made the state finals by default. Consequently, no one knew how this brand-new team would play against an experienced program.

Ironically, 1951 was also the year a state university was taken to federal court for preventing a Black student from entering its law school. Gregory Swanson had all the qualifications for admission, except the color of his skin. He was represented by none other than Thurgood Marshall, a future titan of the U.S. Supreme Court and one of the most respected jurists who ever lived. The school lost on appeal and the prevailing lawyer and his client made history.

Meanwhile, Norton's Little League sponsors and coaches refused to eject their Black players and would have won the state title by forfeiture had the segregated team failed to show. Instead, Charlottesville came to Norton to pummel the mixed-race upstarts, and lost 12-3.

The game was preceded by a Main Street parade attended by 1,400 local supporters, Black and White alike, all pulling together.

Only in Hollywood and the Appalachian coalfields could this epic underdog victory have happened in that very widespread racist era.

The first photo below is of the team sponsored by the Norton Lion's Club, and the next picture catches the state champion team boarding what was likely their first airplane ride. As of 2022, the Black players, Harold Mitchell and Johnny Blair, are survived by six of their White teammates. The Blue Ridge PBS of Roanoke, Virginia, is filming a documentary of the team at my urging. Whether it will be completed remains to be seen.

So coalfield Virginia became the first locality in the entire South to embrace players of color—think about that. It is high time for our nation to hear stories of Appalachia other than chronic distress, desperation, and destitution.

Norton Lion's Club sponsored team

Norton's state championship Little League team on their way to play the West Virginia state champions.

More than a decade earlier, in neighboring Russell County, Virginia, the 1938-39 Dante Central High School football team became the first public high school in the *nation* to integrate sports (if a thorough Google search is considered reliable evidence).

Dante (pronounced *Daint* locally) was a built-from-scratch unincorporated coal town replete with a coal-fired power plant, public water system, brand new housing, a company general store, cafés, movie house, schools, and churches, all provided by the Clinchfield Coal Company.

Interestingly, and a prime example of out-of-state speculators buying Appalachian coal property, Stilson Hutchins, the founder of the *Washington Post*, purchased 4,000 acres in that region in the very early 1900s for $18.00 per acre. After failing miserably at coal mining, he sold out to an experienced Virginia investor, George Lafayette Carter, who went on to create thousands of coal and railroading jobs throughout Southwest Virginia and nearby West Virginia.

The housing in Dante (and most Appalachian coal company towns) was separated by coal companies so that Black sharecroppers from the South, as well as Italian, Slovak, Hungarian, Greek and other immigrants, could live in their own mini-neighborhoods within this overall very diverse community of 3,500 men, women, and children. The public schools were indeed segregated by state law. Yet the coalfields offered many opportunities for these impoverished sharecroppers and immigrants not available in most of the nation.

Coal companies had various motives for separating the races and nationalities from the predominantly White Appalachian native population throughout the coalfield towns and camps. Some company bosses feared the residents would clash, and others did not want union efforts to gain a foothold; therefore, a separated community seemed like a good defense. Most company speculators, owners, and officials came from northern environs where natural or politically arranged settlement patterns in their cities ended up being segregated.

Nonetheless, the coalfield camps and towns were small enough and the houses close enough to promote contact among diverse neighbors. This close proximity worked well for strong interrelationships and unionizing.

FRANK KILGORE

Integrated Dante High School Football Team, 1938-39

Closer view of members of the integrated Dante High School Football Team, 1938-39

Seagon Hollow, 1916

The town of Dante image above with the hand-printed title "Colored Town" is on the face of a 1916 *real photo* postcard. The company gave this section of town the formal name of Seagon Hollow, but according to elders long passed on, the town residents, both White and Black, preferred the nicknames Sawmill Hollow or Colored Town.

The term "Colored Town" is awkward to repeat nowadays but, just like the NAACP (National Association for the Advancement of Colored People) of today, the historical names of people, places, and things should be considered in juxtaposition to what was accepted at the time, not necessarily by today's ever-changing standards.

The second floor of the two-story church building shown in the postcard hosted a school for the sharecroppers' children and grandchildren until a new brick school, named Arty-Lee, was built a few decades later. The coal company officials in Dante resided in much larger houses on Roanoke Hill, snidely referred to by locals, again White and Black, as "snob knob."

One theory as to how White and Black miners and their families got along so well is that their wages, particularly in unionized companies, were basically the same pay for the same work and experience.

Dante school teacher and her students, 1940 (Note the pride and love in her face)

Downtown Dante, 1930s

Clinchfield Inn, Dante

The Clinchfield Company Store

A 1930s typical native Appalachian coalfield "farm"

In fact, coal town Black and immigrant residents usually had better housing and amenities than many native Whites, as depicted in the photo above.

Native coalfield Whites usually bought or inherited land, albeit steep and thin-soiled, outside of coal towns and camps. This allowed subsistence farming that minimally fed their families during routine lay-offs and union recruitment efforts that prompted some coal companies to blackball union sympathizers. Yet many native mountaineers preferred "town life" and abandoned their hardscrabble ancestral farmsteads to become part of a thriving multi-racial, multicultural, and multi-faceted community.

As for better wages, Dr. Ronald Lewis of West Virginia University points out that a Black sharecropper in the 1920s was paid once a year and averaged seventy-five cents to one dollar a day working and living on southern farms. In comparison, while working in the Appalachian coalfields, they and their native and immigrant co-workers averaged $3.20 to $7.40 per day for an eight-hour shift, depending upon skills and experience. Imagine the allure of 300-700 percent pay raises, new houses with indoor plumbing, and a much greater freedom of association. Coal company labor recruiters went to great lengths to seek and retain experienced miners from Western and Eastern Europe, as well as unskilled workers from the South.

This equity of wages was not the custom of the day for African Americans and certain immigrant industrial and service workers in other parts of America; Irish and Italian peoples specifically coming to mind.

This "equal pay for equal work" tendency in the coalfields provided financial parity and dignity to immigrants and Black miners alike, at least within their own homes and communities.

CHAPTER 3
WE'RE MORE MULTI-RACIAL THAN YOU MAY THINK!
THE MELUNGEONS

The Melungeons

OTHER PEOPLE of diverse racial and cultural roots have lived in Appalachia since the mid-1700s, mainly in the mountain regions of east Tennessee and southwest Virginia. They are referred to as Melungeons, and for centuries their origins were quite a mystery until modern DNA technology partially settled the debate.

Some theorists, including many people of Melungeon descent, have previously opined that this dark-complexioned and unique mixed-race Appalachian population emanated from Portuguese forays into very early America. Another theory holds that they are descendants of Turkish prisoners of war left behind by Spanish merchants. Others speculate that they emerged from Jewish origins, including the Lost Tribes of Israel. However, for eons the most popular local theory, and one that still lingers, has been that they are Whites mixed with Cherokee and other Native American tribes.

The highest concentration of these mysterious mountain citizens is in the Clinch River Valley, with its headwaters in Tazewell County, Virginia. This famously bio-diverse river courses southwest through Northeast Tennessee to the Tennessee River and beyond.

Ironically, some Cherokee scholars also believe that their tribe's DNA includes Jewish blood, and even DNA testing has not completely settled that theory. According to National Geographic, testing in 2013 indicated markers of Middle Eastern blood among some Native Americans. Various proponents of this Jewish lineage theory even speculate that King Solomon may have reached what is now America during his three-year trading voyages to bring gold and exotic animals back to Israel.

Many Melungeon bloodlines, according to multiple DNA projects, are made up of more than two races, and researchers categorize this fascinating population as a tri-racial-isolate group. Prior to DNA markers being identified, everything about their history was hotly debated, even how they came to be called Melungeons.

The name itself may have first been applied by a Frenchman attempting to start a French settlement in Virginia west of the Clinch River in the early 1900s. Francois Pierre De Tubeuf was having difficulties with squatters of dark complexions on his huge new estate. Clearly they were not Native American, otherwise, Pierre would have likely lost his scalp. He is said to have referred to the mixed-race residents on his land as *mélange*, meaning *a mixture* in French. So, it is plausible that given his struggles with the English language, he resorted to this French term to indicate that his tormentors were of a mixed race.

However, the more likely theory is that the name came from the Portuguese language, given that Portugal was an early slave-trading country that hired African mercenaries (and alleged cannibals) to abduct thousands of men, women, and children in Angola and surrounding tribal lands on the west coast of Africa. That may explain why many generations of Melungeons claimed to be of Portuguese descent, since that was their African ancestors' last place of residence prior to being shipped to the New World.

A more thorough thesis of that history is found in an article entitled "MALUNGU: The African Origin of the American Melungeons," written by Tim Hashaw. This 2001 publication is accessible online at *Eclectic Magazine*, which earns its name for scouting out unique authors and topics. It is a fascinating story of Black freemen having much more portability and citizen rights than the actual slaves that came afterwards, particularly in Virginia.

Many coal counties in Appalachia have long standing settlements of Melungeons going back to the mid-1700s. They usually situated their communities in the least farmable and most remote places in the mountains. There are several reasons for this tendency: the mountainous, sparsely populated land was much more affordable and available to a racially diverse group that had been held back by racist state laws and poverty; they desired to live amongst their own kind in isolated places for support and protection (tribalism); and they shared the fear that their potential African blood would cause even more discrimination. It is just as feasible that the Melungeons themselves were not certain of their various racial lineages.

It is written that Eastern Virginia slave runners would sometimes kidnap Melungeon children born of freeman parents to sell to plantation owners. If so, no fear on Earth could match that sin. So it was that freed people of color and other minorities came by foot or wagon to the Appalachian frontier for cheap land, job opportunities, protection, and social freedom. Occasionally these treks were also motivated by moderate-to-severe brushes with the law.

The non-coal counties of Hancock and Hawkins are located in the mountains of Northeast Tennessee, and are well known for having the largest populations per capita of Melungeon bloodlines in the nation. Their offspring and other relatives spread throughout the coalfield mountains as they pressed, or were pressed, ever westward into Appalachia's most remote venues. DNA results show that these mysterious Americans are mostly of European and African descent and not so much Native Americans or Middle Easterners, as has been posited by a variety of authors.

Thousands of Appalachian people of all colors, including white, claim to be part Native American (particularly Cherokee). No doubt Native Americans were part of a small trace of the Melungeon DNA results, but more likely this vigorous claim was an attempt to avoid the restrictions foisted upon bi- and tri-racial people by state laws before, during, and after the Civil War. For instance, in 1924 Virginia adopted the Racial Integrity Act to base one's race whether one had "one drop of blood" of African origin. Jim Crow laws also taught dark-complexioned citizens to claim any race except Black.

The coalfield mountains' public school systems had mixed-race students way before the rest of the nation. Although Tennessee officially did not allow Melungeons to vote, and church missionaries constructed separate schools for those children of color such as the Vardy Community School in Hancock County, there was no way these racist states could fully enforce their vicious laws in the communities that had already commingled for decades. The coalfield area of Southwest Virginia had many Melungeon students on the roster when I was in grade school starting in 1958. Their surnames are found in many public-school yearbooks in our coalfield communities. Their lives were not all rosy, but the majority of poor kids around the world get the cold shoulder, despite their racial makeup.

In 1960, a bi-racial family lived very near the school, and the father was the town's fire chief for decades. His children were schooled as all of us were, and perhaps received special treatment because their dad was loved by all. Basically, the ultra-racist Virginia majority at that time simply did not mess with us. Maybe it's because we are far away from the state capitol (reportedly we are closer to six out-of-state legislative bodies) or, as now, pretty much ignored by Richmond and investors. Take your pick.

As generations of Melungeons went by, the European stock took a majority hold of the local DNA. Before that era, most of these fascinating Americans were much more darkly complexioned people than now. The Melungeons that settled in isolated areas of Appalachia were some of the earliest pioneers to do so, which gave them a wink-and-nod pass on the racial scale. Just as many White citizens of those remote mountains stayed with the Union during the Civil War, they also mixed and matched with their dark-skinned land-hungry neighbors and became the fabric of the area. Although Melungeons suffered some discrimination in Appalachia, it was nothing like mid and western Tennessee and eastern and central Virginia's all-out hatred toward "one drop of blood" Americans.

The History and Culture of Coalfields Southwest Virginia

A 1989 scholarly article documenting the influx of sharecroppers to the coalfield culture was authored by Dr. Ronald Lewis, professor at West Virginia University, entitled "From Peasant to Proletarian: The Migration of Southern Blacks to the Central Appalachian Coalfields." It is a must-read, fortunately accompanied by the following multi-state comparative census chart.

BLACK POPULATION OF CENTRAL APPALACHIA
1860–1980

	Kentucky	Tennessee	Virginia	West Virginia	Totals
1860	5,814	2,175	3,405	3,769	15,163
1870	4,941	2,254	3,885	3,280	14,360
1880	6,734	2,570	4,242	5,781	19,327
1890	7,444	3,653	6,552	12,577	30,226
1900	7,602	3,609	7,056	21,584	39,851
1910	10,222	4,415	7,669	41,945	64,251
1920	15,692	2,943	8,953	60,488	88,076
1930	18,286	2,129	7,616	80,841	108,872
1940	18,662	1,918	7,709	85,465	113,754
1950	14,284	2,941	6,659	86,421	110,305
1960	10,240	2,884	4,083	64,613	81,820
1970	7,232	2,718	2,585	44,956	57,491
1980	6,506	3,253	2,688	42,277	54,724

SOURCE: U. S. Bureau of the Census, *Characteristics of the Population* for the decennial censuses of 1860 through and including 1980. For the counties included in central Appalachia see note 5.

The recent U.S. Census population tally does not identify people of Melungeon descent as Black or any race other than White. In fact, the current demographic statistics of Hawkins and Hancock counties in Tennessee do not mention the mixed racial make-up which, if accurately counted, would likely prove that a bi- and tri-racial majority resides there instead of the official count of ninety-seven percent White. In regard to racial diversity, the Appalachian counties having large generational populations of Melungeons as embedded citizens could per capita rival most U.S. rural jurisdictions and numerous cities for racial diversity.

www.loc.gov/pictures/item/2006677596/ The most notable persons of allegedly Melungeon descent are Abraham Lincoln and Elvis (no last name needed).

Surely these overlooked Appalachians, dating back more than two centuries, should be celebrated as part of our nation's overall heritage so they can finally come in out of the cold. Employment and educational opportunities for their progeny would be greatly, and deservedly, enhanced.

From my decades of personal experience working with, representing, and studying the ever-changing theories of the origins of the Melungeon people, it is worth noting that in the coalfields our citizens of Melungeon descent were treated more liberally and fairly than those living in the mostly timbering and farming communities farther to the east.

Since their arrival in the coalfields, many have held, and presently hold, elective offices and are generational leaders in every aspect of coalfield society. Working together in the region's biggest (and historically the world's most dangerous) extractive industry and sharing those experiences and collective struggles garnered many positive and inclusive effects.

This European, sharecropper, and Melungeon melting pot in coalfield Appalachia rivaled New York City in the varieties of diverse populations and proportions. Membership in the United Mine Workers of America (UMWA) peaked at nearly one million miners during the era spanning 1890-1940. Blacks, immigrants, and their progeny were numerous and some of the most dedicated members and supporters of the union.

Imagine coming from a sharecropping family living in abject poverty replete with shanties and little access to education, medical care, or respect. Or ponder the immigrants whose first wave of settlers could not speak or write English. For example, a century ago a huge underground methane gas explosion near Pocahontas, Virginia, killed so many recently employed immigrant miners that a new cemetery was established. Their grave markers were inscribed in their native languages.

After some acclimation, the progeny of these risk-takers found much greater freedom of association, a strong union, and a better quality of life. By working side by side with White and Melungeon natives, they also forged bonds of brotherhood and community relationships.

One of the many fascinating markers in the cemetery in Pocahontas, Virginia

In the 1920s, Wise County, Virginia, with 46,500 residents (eight percent African American, not counting the Melungeon population), was the second most populated county in the entire state. The county's 1928 school board summary report below shows the rapid increase of population during the most accelerated coal-boom days and the growing number of foreign-born citizens settling in for new opportunities.

The following immigration statistic is somewhat misleading regarding the total numbers of nationalities present, in that their American-born children were counted as White population natives, which most of them surely were. It's a given that the large family households of that era likely had multiple times more children in their households than their immigrant parents' numbers indicate.

Children and grandchildren born of these early-century migrants increased in numbers substantially until the 1950s, when coal mining automation forced a mass exodus of natives and non-natives alike. Tens of thousands were laid off (approximately one-third of the coal mining labor workforce), and the working-age heads of households, with families in tow, headed to the steel mills and automobile factories "up north."

THE COUNTY OF WISE

Foreign-born

The foreign-born white population in Wise County for 1920 is distributed as follows:

Country	Number
Armenia	5
Austria	32
Canada	18
Czecho-slovaki	1
Denmark	1
England	34
France	1
Germany	16
Greece	6
Hungary	396
Ireland	8
Italy	107
Netherlands	2
Poland	73
Russia	28
Scotland	9
Sweden	3
Switzerland	1
Syria	27
Wales	3
All other countries	7

VITAL STATISTICS
II

Birth Rates in Wise County (1913-1926)

Year	Per 1,000 Total Population	Per 1,000 Total Population	Per 1,000 Total Population
1913	42.4	47.3	20.8
1914	40.1	41.5	44.6
1915	37.8	39.2	21.9
1916	34.4	40.8	23.1
1917	38.7	39.5	27.0
1918	30.2		
1919	41.9		
1920	40.8	42.4	23.6
1921	48.1	49.6	32.1
1922	40.6	41.9	24.7
1923	45.1	45.9	35.4
1924	43.0	44.4	27.5
1925	35.34	36.75	19.54
1926	31.91	33.06	19.11
Average	39.31	41.85	26.60

Death Rates in Wise County (1913-1926)

Year	Per 1,000 Total Population	Per 1,000 Total Population	Per 1,000 Total Population
1913	14.4	14.0	19.6
1914	12.3	11.5	21.1
1915	10.0	9.5	15.9
1916	12.7	12.7	
1917	13.2	13.1	
1918	15.0		
1919	12.7		
1920	13.4	12.9	19.7
1921	11.4	11.0	16.4
1922	10.2	9.7	16.0
1923	12.5	11.5	24.1
1924	10.9	10.2	18.3
1925	9.66	9.29	13.86
1926	10.42	9.92	16.0
Average	12.05	11.27	18.09

Marriages and Divorces in Wise County (1918-1926)

Year	Total Number of Marriages	Total White Marriages	Total Colored Marriages	Total Number Divorces	Number Marriages to each Divorce
1918	520	362	158	58	8.97
1919	634	488	145	105	6.04
1920	660	503	157	89	7.42
1921	555	441	114	95	5.84
1922	553	437	116	65	8.50
1923	660	534	126	80	8.25
1924	426	373	53	59	7.22
1925	407	341	66	66	6.17
1926	481	408	73	57	8.44
Average	544	431	112	74	7.42

Information about residents of Wise County from 1913 to 1926, including foreign-born residents

1920 Hungarian funeral, Preacher Creek, Wise County, Virginia

So, it is not clear whether the integrated Norton Little League and Dante football teams were unlikely social experiments, a matter of temporary necessity, or that it was just locally accepted that young Black students (whose schools did not field such teams at the time) simply wanted to play baseball and football with their White coal-town buddies. What is certain is that the teammates' fathers worked closely together in very tight quarters and dangerous conditions.

Maybe the unique coalfields spirit of inclusiveness arose from the logic of survival, in that it was simply not a good idea to hate, or be hated by, the miner next to you who might be, in a flash, called upon to save your life from the various gruesome ways one can die underground.

In those days (and for decades prior to and afterwards), tens of thousands of miners each year were killed or permanently disabled by rock falls, methane gas explosions, underground flooding, electrocutions, and equipment failures. Though rare, miners working at the face of a coal seam could collapse in a split second from asphyxiation as the 200-million-year-old exposed carbon literally sucked the oxygen from the immediate mine interior, a terrifying condition known as "black damp."

If these traumatic events didn't take a miner out of service and into poverty, ever-present chronic black lung disease caused by inhaling coal and rock dust awaited, guaranteeing a miserable, lingering, premature demise via "smothering to death."

Cherry Mine Disaster, RPPC, 259 Miners and Trapper Boys died in that fire. Cherry, Illinois, 1909. Courtesy of Earl Dotter.

Coal mining was one of the most deadly occupations in the nation until enhanced federal safety laws, adopted in 1969, improved the health and safety of miners who were previously endangered by very weak national and state safety standards. Prior attempts to save lives and limbs were too often dictated by coal company influence rather than practical, humane considerations.

As an example of the slow evolution of coal mine safety, the first federal control of coal mining was passed in 1891. In a huge leap for the time, children under the age of twelve could no longer work in the mines within the U.S. Territories.

Fraternal organizations such as the Loyal Order of Moose (circa 1888) financially assisted their fellow injured miners (or their survivors). The companies and individual coal states often lagged behind these private humanitarian efforts until the federal government finally stepped in, with gusto, eighty years later.

Contrary to assumptions, Appalachia was not the first region in the nation to produce commercial coal. That title goes to the relatively small coal-bearing areas of Richmond, Virginia, as captioned below.

The small Midlothian coal field was valuable to the local market, and was exported to Caribbean islands. The coal was valued for its ability to provide heat, and reportedly was used in the White House fireplaces when Thomas Jefferson was president. More than coal brought out of Midlothian, the James River and Appomattox River waterpower was a greater factor in the development of manufacturing at Richmond and Petersburg.[4]

37 men were killed in the 1882 explosion of a Midlothian coal mine, after methane accumulated in the poorly-ventilated tunnels
Source: Virginia Commonwealth University, James Branch Cabell Library, The fatal explosion at the Midlothian Coal Mine

Coal was also mined in Henrico County, west of Richmond.

TABLE 6.07 Coal Mining History: 1761 to 1924				
Name	Origin	Date Closed	Depth (in feet)	General Location
Carbon Hill District				
Saunders Shaft	Early 1800s	1902	220	Near intersection of Lauderdale Dr. and Causeway Dr.
Eureka Shaft	1853	Unknown	230	Near intersection of Lauderdale Dr. and Francis Drake Dr.
Turpius Colliery, Magruder Pit, Maggi Pit	Pre-Civil War	Unknown	Unknown	West of Poplar Forest Dr.
Gayton Shaft, Coke Shaft, Orchard Shaft, Twin Shaft, Double Shaft, Breaker Shaft	Pre-1819	1901	325	SW of intersection of Gayton Rd. and Ridgefield Pkwy.
Edge Hill Shaft	Around 1842	Unknown	264	Near intersection of Poplar Forest Dr. and Taft Pl.
Barbershop Shaft, Railroad Shaft	Unknown	Unknown	Unknown	Near intersection of Gayton Rd. and Milhaven Dr.
Deep Shaft, Air or Shelter Air Shaft, Snead's Shaft, Crouch and Snead's Shaft, Crouche's Pits, Brooks Shaft	Around 1851	1875	200	8E of intersection of Lauderdale Dr. and Westshire Ln.
Coalbrook Slope, Trent Slope, Jos. R. Anderson and Company Mine, Carbon Hill Mine, Old Dominion Development Co. No. 1 Mine, Mule Shaft, Engine Shaft	Around 1848	1903	over 300	SW of intersection of Lauderdale Dr. and John Rolfe Pkwy.
Cottrell's Pits	Around 1835	1841	Unknown	South of Coalbrook Slope
Deep Run District				
Deep Run Pits, Springfield Pits, Duvall's Pits, Burton's Pits, Roxx and Curry Pits, Barr's Pits	Pre-1761	1924	Unknown	NW of intersection of W. Broad St. and Gaskins Rd.

DECADES BEFORE PRESENT-DAY mining became highly mechanized, the equipment used came in many forms and unsafe varieties, such as the wooden-wheeled cart shown below, used to haul coal from the mines to a rudimentary tipple. These homemade do-it-yourself solutions were common in the smaller mining operations. While showing some ingenuity, the equipment designers were obviously not particularly worried about safety. A more "modern" (circa 1940s) version of a coal tipple is shown as well.

(A) View of simple improvised tipple used at many local mines. Note the wooden axles, wheels, and track and the utilization of the fork of a tree at the end of the tipple proper to check the car as it is thrown forward in dumping. As a study in evolution compare this simple though effective arrangement with the highly specialized modern tipples shown below.

(B) Tipple and loading track of the Hamlin Coal Company at Hamlin, Va.

Coal Mining Death Count

Year	Miners	Fatalities	Year	Miners	Fatalities	Year	Miners	Fatalities	Year	Miners	Fatalities
1900	448,581	1,489	1930	644,006	2,063	1960	189,679	325	1990	168,625	66
1901	485,544	1,574	1931	589,705	1,463	1961	167,568	294	1991	158,677	61
1902	518,197	1,724	1932	527,623	1,207	1962	161,286	289	1992	153,128	55
1903	566,260	1,926	1933	523,182	1,064	1963	157,126	284	1993	141,183	47
1904	593,693	1,995	1934	566,426	1,226	1964	150,761	242	1994	143,645	45
1905	626,045	2,232	1935	565,202	1,242	1965	148,734	259	1995	132,111	47
1906	640,780	2,138	1936	584,582	1,342	1966	145,244	233	1996	126,451	39
1907	680,492	3,242	1937	589,856	1,413	1967	139,312	222	1997	126,429	30
1908	690,438	2,445	1938	541,528	1,105	1968	134,467	311	1998	122,083	29
1909	666,552	2,642	1939	539,375	1,078	1969	133,302	203	1999	114,489	35
1910	725,030	2,821	1940	533,267	1,388	1970	144,480	260	2000	108,098	38
1911	728,348	2,656	1941	546,692	1,266	1971	142,108	181	2001	114,458	42
1912	722,662	2,419	1942	530,861	1,471	1972	162,207	156	2002	110,966	28
1913	747,644	2,785	1943	486,516	1,451	1973	151,892	132	2003	104,824	30
1914	763,185	2,454	1944	453,937	1,298	1974	182,274	133	2004	108,734	28
1915	734,008	2,269	1945	437,921	1,068	1975	224,412	155	2005	116,436	23
1916	720,971	2,226	1946	463,079	968	1976	221,255	141	2006	122,975	47
1917	757,317	2,696	1947	490,356	1,158	1977	237,506	139	2007	122,936	34
1918	762,426	2,580	1948	507,333	999	1978	255,588	106	2008	133,828	30
1919	776,569	2,323	1949	485,306	585	1979	260,429	144	2009	134,089	18
1920	784,621	2,272	1950	483,239	643	1980	253,007	133	2010	135,500	48
1921	823,253	1,995	1951	441,905	785	1981	249,738	153	2011	143,437	20
1922	844,807	1,984	1952	401,329	548	1982	241,454	122	2012	137,650	20
1923	862,536	2,462	1953	351,126	461	1983	200,199	70	2013	123,259	20
1924	779,613	2,402	1954	283,705	396	1984	208,160	125	2014	116,010	16
1925	748,805	2,518	1955	260,089	420	1985	197,049	68	2015	102,804	12
1926	759,033	2,234	1956	260,285	448	1986	185,167	89	2016	81,485	8
1927	759,177	2,231	1957	254,725	478	1987	172,780	63	2017	82,843	15
1928	682,831	2,176	1958	224,890	358	1988	166,278	53	2018	82,699	12
1929	654,494	2,187	1959	203,597	293	1989	164,929	68	2019	81,361	12

Approximately 100,000 coal miners from dozens of countries, southern sharecroppers, native Melungeons, and Whites died in the United States in the 20th Century alone. Note that fatalities decreased significantly following implementation of the 1969 federal safety guidelines as indicated above.

CHAPTER 4
THE LEADERSHIP ROLES OF WOMEN IN OUR COALFIELDS AND THE MOUNTAIN LEADERS WHO SUPPORTED THEM

IN ADDITION to racial and ethnic minorities, women also earned opportunities and benefited from coalfield open-mindedness. Even before the Virginia coalfields definitively broke the color barrier in Dante and Norton, Helen Timmons Henderson in 1923 became one of the first of two women to win seats to the state legislature. This long-overdue civil right came about three years after the 19th Amendment to the U.S. Constitution allowed over half of the nation's adult population to vote for the first time.

Helen and her husband helped establish the Baptist Mountain School in Buchanan County, one of the most prolific coal-producing counties in the state. She was nominated to run again but passed away before the election. Her daughter, Helen Ruth Henderson, succeeded her late mother and worked tirelessly for better education and roads for her adopted mountain homeland.

Not only did coalfield voters elect two women legislators within one decade, but both were "outsiders" from Missouri. These elections should also debunk our reputation for hating outsiders. (Alert! The novel and movie *Deliverance* are not documentaries.)

These elected female officials got things done and were much loved and respected due to their unbridled devotion to children, education, and improved transportation.

Helen Timmons Henderson

Mrs. Walter Colquitt Fain, left and Mrs. Robert Anderson Henderson, first women to be elected to the Virginia General Assembly.
—Photo by Staff Photographer.

First Women Elected To General Assembly Guests At Reception

Norfolk Pays Homage To Her Own Mrs. Fain And To Mrs. Henderson, of Southwest Virginina, On Eve of Their Departure For Richmond.

ALTHOUGH OUR FOREFATHERS and mothers were taken advantage of by natural-resource speculators who made sure our wealth was exported to cities far away, there were other outsiders who came to the aid of women and children in our region in an effort to enhance their access to education and jobs. These missionaries established schools and work opportunities, provided shelter from domestic violence, and gave encouragement to mountain women and their children. They also advocated for legislation to reduce coal mining injuries and deaths, and to offer a safety net for families of killed or disabled coal miners.

Outdoor sermon at Grace House on the Mountain, Wise County, 1940s

Honey Branch Chapel, 1940, where Wise, Russell, and Dickenson counties merge. Reverend Leonell and Deaconess Booth Brereton.

Grace House on the Mountain Episcopal Mission of the Diocese of Southwest Virginia, built in the early 1920s. Miss Margaretha Williamson, worker, Miss Nellie Kilgore, and her father, John W. Kilgore, rural mail carrier on horseback.

As for supporting women, the following achievement is literally unheralded: during the state's 246-year history, only six women have been elected to the Supreme Court of Virginia by the Virginia General Assembly. Interestingly, three of them (yes, half) are from coalfield Virginia, and each had as her primary sponsor Delegate Terry Kilgore, a Scott County farm boy who recently made his way to the majority leader of the Virginia House of Delegates.

Cynthia Kinser of Lee County stands as the first and only woman to become a Chief Justice of the Court. Although this dearth of female justices is an abomination, the three coalfield women members of that Court come from Virginia's last frontier and the heartland of the so-called Hillbilly Firewall. Not bad considering the extremely small population in the mountains compared to the state's more thriving communities.

Left to right: Now retired Justices Elizabeth McClanahan and Cynthia Kinser, and then court of appeals Judge Teresa Chafin, from the coalfield counties of Buchanan, Lee, and Russell, respectively.

Justice McClanahan subsequently served as Dean of the Appalachian School of Law in her native Buchanan County, an institution I was honored to help establish. (Disclosure: the author is the proud spouse of Justice Chafin, who worked her way up the ranks from juvenile court, the circuit trial court, the state's court of appeals, and ultimately to the Supreme Court of Virginia.)

Virginia Supreme Court Justice Teresa Chafin

And speaking of the Appalachian School of Law, it might be a surprise, or more likely a shock, to the nation's negative notions of our region to learn that it consistently has the most diverse law school student body in the state, as the photo and stats below demonstrate.

Faculty, staff and student leaders of the Appalachian School of Law

Diversity Statistics for Appalachian School of Law October 2019				
	1L Students	2L Students	3L Students	Overall Student Body
White	43/72 (59.72%)	33/43 (76.74%)	30/49 (61.22%)	106/164 (64.63%)
Black	7/72 (9.72%)	2/43 (4.65%)	11/49 (22.45%)	20/164 (12.20%)
Hispanic	10/72 (13.89%)	0/43 (0%)	3/49 (6.12%)	13/164 (7.93%)
Asian	3/72 (4.17%)	4/43 (9.30%)	2/49 (4.08%)	9/164 (5.49%)
American Indian	3/72 (4.17%)	1/43 (2.33%)	1/49 (2.04%)	5/164 (3.05%)
Non-Resident Alien	3/72 (4.17%)	0/43 (0%)	0/49 (0%)	3/164 (1.83%)
Unknown	3/72 (4.17%)	3/43 (6.98%)	2/49 (4.08%)	8/164 (4.88%)
Non-White	23/72 (31.94%)	7/43 (16.28%)	17/49 (34.69%)	47/164 (28.66%)

Appalachian School of Law White: 69.2% Black: 12.3% Hispanic: 4.1% Asian: 5.5%	**Marshall-Wythe School of Law** White: 75.8% Black: 6.7% Hispanic: 4.2% Asian: 3.9%
Antonin Scalia Law School White: 74.8% Black: 2.0% Hispanic: 7.7% Asian: 7.2%	**Washington & Lee University** White: 75.3% Black: 5.1% Hispanic: 4.5% Asian: 6.8%
University of Richmond School of Law White: 73.5% Black: 6.6% Hispanic: 1.3% Asian: 3.2%	**Regent University School of Law** White: 75.7% Black: 7.2% Hispanic: 7.2% Asian: 3.2%
Liberty University School of Law White: 75.8% Black: 4.8% Hispanic: 6.8% Asian: 3.2%	**University of Virginia School of Law** White: 74% Black: 5.7% Hispanic: 5.2% Asian: 6.8%

*All statistics are from American Bar Association disclosures and can be found on: http://www.abarequireddisclosures.org/Disclosure509.aspx

If readers are surprised, and I hope better informed, by this list of firsts found in just our little corner of the Appalachian coalfields, then that is true progress.

But wait, I have another gem to share regarding the Virginia coalfields and opportunities for women's rights. The Slemp family has a 170-plus-year history of coalfield-bred public service from the state legislature and office of presidential secretary to the U.S. Congress. Charles "Chuck" Slemp is the most recent public servant of the family and served as Chief Deputy Virginia Attorney General until June 1, 2024. Obviously this family of generational patriots has made our coalfield heritage shine.

Campbell Slemp held a state legislative seat with the then-racist and sexist Democratic majority political party before switching to the Republican side, the more progressive party at that time. He won a hard-fought seat in the U.S. Congress in 1902, becoming the only progressive member of the state's national representatives.

His son, C. Bascom, succeeded him and was the only Virginia congressman to support the 19th Amendment to the U.S. Constitution—the law of the land that allowed women to vote. Every Congressional member of Virginia's majority party voted no. Some sources claim that Congressman Slemp was the only pro-women congressional vote in the entire South. Hopefully that is not accurate.

This unique history is proof beyond a reasonable doubt that coalfield residents march to a different drum in all realms of fairness, especially when compared to many parts of the nation. Even today, in the Slemp tradition, the Virginia coalfields send pragmatic state legislators to Richmond.

My great Uncle Wilse told me one time that he liked his politicians the way he liked his steaks, medium. We proudly send firefighters, not flamethrowers, to the state capitol. Hopefully that stays the norm.

President Calvin Coolidge (second from left) swearing in C. Bascom Slemp (second from right) as his presidential secretary in 1923. Courtesy of Library of Congress.

DID WE HAVE, and do we have, glaring exceptions to these standouts? Of course we do. But being consistently denigrated for centuries for our alleged stupidity and closed-mindedness is based upon ingrained bias and overt lies. By the way, much of the progressive movement talked about today started here, in coalfield Appalachia.

Despite this long history of inclusion, I am many times called upon to account for racism and sexism in the coalfields by my friends from other sections of the state and up north. I point out, a little defensively I admit, that although Virginia's coal towns and camps were indeed racially segregated, the races and immigrants in most Appalachian mining communities shopped alongside each other, ate where they chose, went to the same movie houses, worked side-by-side in very dangerous conditions every day, and belonged to the same union.

As a self-appointed coalfield historian and an alleged mountain ambassador-of-sorts, I dutifully provide whoever will listen with examples of our egalitarian and independent culture.

One particular fact generally missed by outsiders is that our ancestors represented a sizable pro-Union sentiment before and during the Civil War. This split with the Confederacy took root before coal was commercially mined region-wide, in what is now called coalfield Appalachia. This pro-Union attitude, for a glaring example, resulted in the 1863 formation of present-day coal-bearing West Virginia.

A substantial number of Appalachians and local officials in neighboring East Tennessee counties also rebelled against the South's secession. Consequently, President Lincoln requested that one of his most trusted generals, Oliver O. Howard (the namesake of Howard University), reward them for their loyalty should anything happen to him. The following article says it all.

> **...And in the Civil War**
>
> It is a fact worthy of note that East Tennessee furnished more troops to the Federal army than any section of the Union in proportion to its population. The male population of East Tennessee in 1860 between the ages of 18 and 45 years was 45,000. Out of this population the lowest estimate of troops who joined the Federal army places them at 30,000, the exact number put down in the statistics of the Government is 31,092, besides a large number that joined the Confederate army. This large proportion of troops to the population is explained to some extent by the fact that many joined the army both over and under the legal military age.
>
> ...And history seems to bear out the fact that in all times those people who inhabit mountainous countries are endowed with a lofty spirit of patriotism and loyalty to country, and are the first to respond to its call when menaced by foreign or domestic foes. Hence arises the fact that East Tennessee, and the mountain sections of adjoining States, have always furnished more than their proportion of volunteers in all the wars in which our country has been engaged.
>
>
>
> from *History of the Thirteenth Regiment Tennessee Volunteer Cavalry U.S.A.* by Samuel W. Scott and Samuel P. Angel, 1903. See review of new reprint on page 43.

Obviously, Tennessee's coalfield residents were not just lukewarm about preserving the Union. More than 30,000 of those southern Appalachians joined the Union Army, which reportedly was the highest geographical per-capita ratio of volunteers in the nation. In fact, the very pro-Union, coal-bearing county of Scott seceded from Tennessee, a Confederate state, due to slavery and a strong fealty to the American flag. Though again considered part of Tennessee several years after the end of the Civil War, this very independent county didn't officially rescind their act of secession and "re-join" Tennessee until 1986.

As a result of General Howard's promise kept, Lincoln Memorial University (LMU) was founded decades later just two miles from the Virginia border in the town of Harrogate, Tennessee. Today, that fast-growing private, faith-based school provides mountain students and young people from around the globe with opportunities to become doctors, lawyers, allied healthcare specialists, businessmen and businesswomen, education leaders, and much-needed dentists.

Most fascinating is that LMU's prolific veterinary hospitals and hands-on rotation classes are located in Lee County, Virginia, whose coal mining days are mostly over. However, the 150,000 square feet of graduate degree education is the nation's fastest growing vet program. This grand facility and its students (eighty-percent female) and faculty are creating jobs and rental income in what was at one time the state's poorest county. Higher education creates higher incomes and financial growth, as you will note in any college town.

A Lee County, Virginia, mountain native and eventual LMU graduate, Autry O.V. "Pete" DeBusk lived in a dozen or so coal camps and towns as his father built coal tipples throughout the coalfield region. Pete learned how to get along with strangers as he switched schools every few months. He went on to prosper in the medical-supplies industry and became the originator of dozens of patents in that field, including the world-famous soft boot cast. He is also the chair of the LMU board, and through dedication, visionary zeal, and generosity, this son of the mountains has helped thousands of Appalachian students receive undergraduate and graduate-level educations they likely could not have accessed without his contributions.

Pete, like many of our Appalachian local leaders, was born of a nurturing culture that is very inclusive by nature. He also has very good things to say about The University of Virginia's College at Wise (UVAW) and consistently recruits its undergraduates for LMU's graduate programs. That is another example of coalfield Appalachia's inclusiveness and a friendly, family-oriented culture.

Autry O.V. "Pete" DeBusk

I usually get blank stares from my buddies or participants in leadership programs I address on occasion as I recount these and other ways that we coalfield Appalachians are far different from the stereotypes others are so apt to inhale and repeat. I am not sure if their stares are due to disbelief, awe, or not fully understanding my mountain dialect, but they are painfully hilarious nonetheless.

For example, let's go back to the history-making presidential runs made by our first African American president. Those two elections supply ample evidence to show that racism here in the Appalachian coalfields is not as pervasive as political pundits like to portray.

For example, in Southwest Virginia the 9th Congressional District (at that time) ran 200 miles from Salem westward to the Cumberland Gap. It is conservative territory no doubt, but the past three pre-Hillary Clinton Democratic presidential candidates, Gore, Kerry, and Obama (all three arguably the most liberal U.S. Senators at the time), each garnered about thirty-nine percent of the vote.

And let's not forget Doug Wilder's historic 1989 victory as the nation's first elected African American governor. He won Virginia's governorship by a razor-thin edge but carried five of the seven coalfield counties by margins from four to twelve percent!

Meanwhile, he did not, or barely carried, the more blue-blooded counties. Many political pundits of that time (including the candidate himself) opined that the coalfields supplied him the boost necessary to make history.

Doug Wilder, campaigning in Lee County with a Democrat war horse, Edgar Bacon.

The obvious question then is, if we are such racists here in the Appalachian coalfields, how did Barack Obama pull the same percentage of votes in his first run as did two of the whitest guys in America? It is no big surprise that President Obama did very poorly here in his re-election bid because by that time his attitude toward coal, gun rights, and other hot rural issues were well known.

And Democrat Hillary Clinton did not help her cause when she looked straight into the TV camera and promised to cut out the highest paying blue-collar jobs in the coal region and, at least by implication, averred that coalfield Appalachians were amongst the most deplorable of the deplorables. Imagine if she had said that reporters and journalists were stale-dated due to the Internet, had run their course, and were no longer needed, thank you very much! I am fairly certain that she would not have garnered their majority support either.

What compelled her to commit this blunder just before the election is still a mystery. The best thesis is that overconfidence led her to assume that rural voters were such a distant minority that their votes were not necessary. This resulted in an unearned victory by her struggling opponent. Such statements many times sink a bullish campaign at the last minute. For example, Republican candidate for president Mitt Romney, during a private fundraising event, alleged that forty-nine percent of Americans were on the public dole. Unfortunately for him, many voters took that comment to include all current and retired public employees, military personnel (including veterans), and the impoverished folks on Medicare, Medicaid, and other public subsidies (his real target most likely). That changed the minds of a significant number of those forty-nine percent of voters. Ironically, he garnered less than forty-nine percent in a beatdown by President Obama, coming in at a non-competitive forty-seven percent. Gaffes literally can and do change the trajectory of our nation and the world.

Agree with the coalfield majority's stance on these hot-button issues or not, the ninety-two-percent-White voting bloc in Virginia's Ninth Congressional District gave President Obama his equal share of votes until it became clear how he felt about us "clinging" to firearms, Bibles, the American flag, and life-sustaining jobs. Voting no to his second term after these revelations was based upon fact-driven microeconomics and democracy, not so much racism. And how did Governor Wilder prevail in his historic coalfield campaign if we were, and are, the knuckle-dragging Neanderthals depicted on both coasts?

In other words, our coalfield region had a history of inclusion way before more genteel regions of the nation and Virginia were ordered by courts to do so. Court-ordered public-school integration in the coalfields was relatively seamless, while some rabidly racist Virginia jurisdictions farther east and north privatized public schools and launched vile litigation in a vain attempt to avoid the federal laws of the land. It took decades in these same radical communities of the state to reach near-full compliance. Even today, very worried old-timey liberals are concerned that our nation's most progressive cities and colleges have backslid toward more-segregated education.

These particular academic and city leaders apparently have forgotten Martin Luther King's life-and-death struggle to not be judged or segregated because of the color of one's skin

CHAPTER 5
EDUCATION AND ATHLETICS

SPEAKING OF SCHOOLS, the notion that Virginia's coalfield residents are impoverished (mostly true) and therefore must be ignorant (a bald-faced lie) needs to be openly addressed. Virginia's 133 school districts are divided by its department of education into regions numbered one through eight. Region 7 is home to all the coalfield counties and the adjacent mountainous agriculture lands to the east, more commonly referred to as Southwest Virginia or the "Great Southwest." (Admittedly, that last moniker may confuse folks; they may end up in Arizona when trying to find us.)

Not so long ago while meeting in Richmond with state and college officials about bringing high-tech jobs to our mining region, I was point-blank asked if our students had the DNA "down there" to handle such sophisticated jobs. After spewing a few visceral comments, I calmed down enough to lay stats on them that debunked such bigotry. My counter-stats went something like this. For the past several years, the students of mountainous Region 7 have scored far above the state public-school average in their Standards of Learning (SOL) tests in math, science, and reading. More than once our young brainiacs bested all other regions, including super-rich Northern Virginia, in these academic achievements.

I literally have friends and family members who doubt that our

Southwest Virginia kids were number one in the state (pre-COVID) regarding public-school academic rankings. That's understandable. Many times the victims of denigration and slander start believing the bad things said about them. This lack of self-confidence is generational in poor communities worldwide. The first step to creating success is getting on the positive side of life in order to counter the trolls.

Let's address in more detail the very harmful outsider assumption that coalfield Appalachian children are "dumber than a sack of hammers." (phrase credited to Ulysses Everett McGill (George Clooney) in the best movie ever, *Oh Brother, Where Art Thou?*)

Wise County, the second-largest coal producer in Virginia, ranked number fourth out of 133 school districts in statewide SOL scores, while super-rich Albemarle County ranked 66th. The state's remaining coalfield counties' pass-rate rankings were as follows: Scott 9th, Tazewell 10th, Russell 13th, Dickenson 16th, and the City of Norton 19th. You get the picture. Only Lee and Buchanan counties lag behind regionally.

> AUTHOR'S NOTE: *These SOL stats are pre-COVID due to the lack of remote-access learning in the outer reaches of rural regions across the nation that grossly skew prior academic outcome; nevertheless, Virginia's Southwest region is making a comeback, and regained first place once again in 2023.*

How can that truly worst-of-all stereotype of "dumbness" be accurate when Southwest Virginia school systems have consistently been number one or two in SOLs in a state that ranks 4th in the nation for the quality of its public school system? Much of coalfield Appalachia has above average academic successes, while some mountain jurisdictions certainly do not. The failing public school systems nationwide suffer mainly from poor adult supervision and leadership. It is rarely the fault of the children. Like young people worldwide, they respond to the environment and encouragement fostered by adults.

It is cruel enough to belittle a state, city, county, or town that is perpetually dragging bottom economically; however, it's even worse to ridicule an impoverished region with top scores in one of the nation's upper-tier public-school systems. Actually, that is defamation, pure and simple.

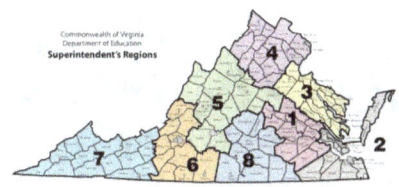

Commonwealth of Virginia Department of Education
Superintendent's Regions

Let the above chart sink in. The second-most-impoverished students in the state with the lowest-paid teachers and highest ratio of special-needs kids have excelled mightily in STEM studies. Our students have also won multiple state championships in drama, forensics, scholastic bowls, robotics (including 7th in the world for coalfield Dickenson County), and some of our schools have reached extremely elite National Blue Ribbon status. In 2024, Ridgeview High School in Dickenson County won the state championship in forensics as did Norton in another category, and the list goes on.

Dickenson County's World Class Robotics Team

Dickenson County's Ridgeview High School champion forensics team

Norton's J.I. Burton High School champion Scholastic Bowl team

Not too long ago one of the coalfield region's nearest non-coal "big" cities, Bristol, Virginia, turned a failing thirty percent minority elementary school from a fifty-six percent SOL pass rate to a ninety-five percent score, garnering a national award. One teacher-turned-principal motivated the kids, their community, and her school board to make magic happen, thereby rescuing many children of color from stereotypical assumptions that they cannot keep pace. Imagine the generational fates of the prior students from that school, including White children of poverty, that did not have sufficient leaders with vision and tenacity.

This inspirational principal, Faith Mabe, born and raised in the coalfields of Wise County, proved beyond a doubt that adult leadership matters and individuals can make a huge difference for kids. This kind of tremendous turnaround can happen almost anywhere with the right motivators that tap the backing of the community, local officials, and the inspired children that depend upon them to lead and care.

The following full-page ad touting our smart young mountaineers was posted by the author in every major newspaper in Virginia.

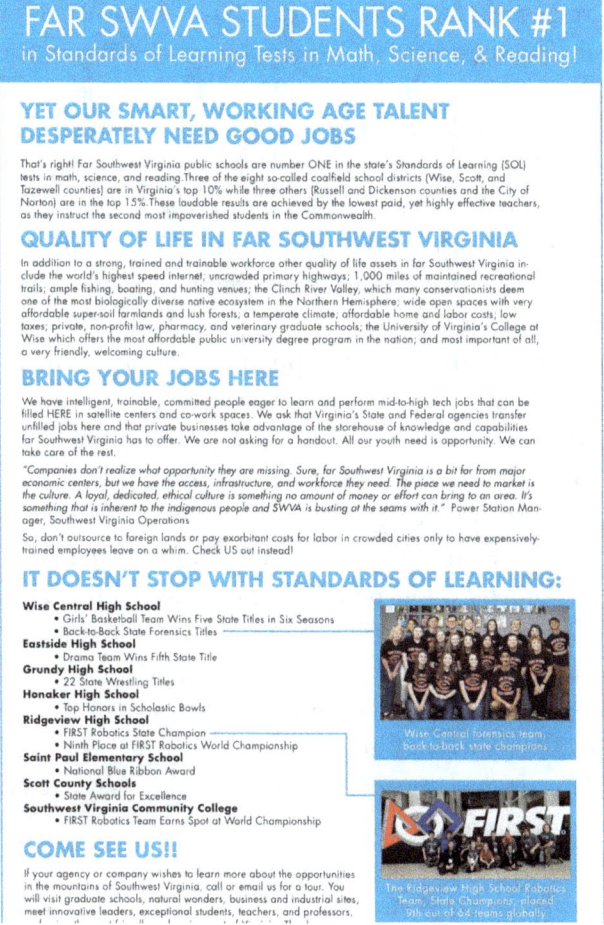

So, what more can and should our young people do to garner respect and coalfield-based job opportunities? We deserve an answer to this bigotry and our kids have earned the opportunity to show the world that they can meet America's expectations.

For a fascinating account of statewide economic disparities, visit www.CardinalNews.org, type in "the numbers we ought to be paying attention to," and review the stat-driven conclusion that **Virginia is the most income-disparate state in the USA** due to hosting the nation's richest communities that border Washington D.C. That stat is then compared to Virginia's rural areas, particularly Southside and the coalfields. The article goes on to posit that keeping our smart young people in rural areas is a good start, but we also need to bring back Appalachian business-driven expatriates and recruit newcomers familiar with working online who are looking for a better way of life. (Courtesy of Dwayne Yancey, editor of Cardinal News)

Dwayne also raises the issue of "How the University of Virginia should use its record endowment." In short, the University of Virginia (UVA) has an endowment of $14.5 BILLION, while its six-plus-decades-old coalfield branch in Wise, Virginia, has yet to offer enough new and expanded graduate-level programs that would create very good jobs and offer other positive opportunities for mountain students and residents. That one move by the mother ship would bring new energy, ideas, and durable prosperity to a chronically poor region, and help fight the harmful stereotype that we are destined to remain poor.

So, it is a constant struggle to whack-a-mole the negative stereotypes that have been hurled our way for decades, even centuries. For example, until prescription opiate drugs seized Middle America, the flooding of powerful painkillers into poor communities such as Appalachia and inner cities was solely blamed on the victims, not Big Pharma. Now the favored diagnoses and remedies have suddenly switched to counseling and understanding that this is a public health crisis mostly caused by greedy drug makers and the few, but deadly, crooked medical professionals in cahoots with them.

When this scourge was raging in poor rural areas and big cities, the solution was jail, prison, and jeering. While it is true that voluntarily taking illegal drugs is ultimately the responsibility of the individual, it is ironic that states are belatedly suing dirty drug companies. Not surprisingly, higher income communities are no longer advocating the "lock-them-up" solution.

As a sidenote, and another point of pride for our mountain region, the U.S. Attorney's office in the Western District of Virginia was the first in the nation to effectively go after drug-pushing Big Pharma. A 2007 case against Purdue Frederick Company and its top executives, prosecuted by Assistant U.S. Attorney Randy Ramseyer, resulted in a

$600 million fine and a corporate felony conviction. Talk about being ahead of the curve!

Yet again, this momentous Appalachian precedent was mostly ignored by national leaders and the media. Cynical Appalachians could rationally suspect that these consistent omissions occur because we are invisible, therefore disposable. But surely not; no enlightened society would be that mean.

I am hesitant to mention the coalfield region's multiple state championships in sports because way too much emphasis is placed on those non-scholastic accomplishments. Yet sports do demonstrate a general toughness and dedication to excel.

Suffice it to say that Buchanan County's seat, Grundy, has won twenty-six high school state champion wrestling trophies as of 2023. The legendary football team state championships produced by the high schools of Appalachia, Big Stone Gap, Clintwood, Gate City, Bluefield, and Richlands also speak for themselves, and that's just the boys!

Meanwhile the Wise Central High School girls' basketball team has won six state titles in the past seven years, and the girls' tennis team boasts ten of Gate City's twenty-seven state titles in a variety of girls' and boys' sports including football, volleyball, softball, and basketball. More recently, the Honaker girls won their third straight basketball state championship to add to Russell County's school achievements. Castlewood High School has earned three baseball championships, plus one softball, one volleyball, one cross-country, and one wrestling title. Lebanon's baseball team took the 2023 state baseball championship under the guidance of longtime Coach Charles "Doc" Adams and the strong arm of pitcher Nathan "Tater" Phillips. Tazewell High School recently won its first softball championship and Dickenson County has captured two. Lee County has three state championships: girls' basketball, boys' football, and golf. And the list goes on and on...

From Ollan Cassell, who ran track for Appalachia High School and later won a 1964 Olympic gold medal in sprinting; to NFL stars Thomas Jones of Big Stone Gap and Heath Miller of Honaker; to fast-ball artist Billy Wagner of Tazewell, the Virginia coalfields have accounted themselves well. These irrefutable stats more than show that coalfield residents are a competitive bunch.

Thomas Jones (Stock photo)

Heath Miller (Courtesy of his proud mother)

Billy Wagner (Stock photo)

Ollan Cassell was honored by the Virginia General Assembly in 2020 as the lead sprinter in the 1964 world record USA 4X400m relay team gold medal event. He went on to become the executive director of the U.S. Track and Field organization and a member of the National Track and Field Hall of Fame. (photo by Donnie Ratliff)

Ollan and his teammates celebrate their world record

Special Tribute:

NFL star Thomas Jones was raised in a coal camp tar-papered house in Appalachia, Virginia, while his mother, Betty, worked in nearby coal mines for twenty years. She was likely the first female coal miner in Virginia, and, if not, she certainly was the first Black woman coal digger; think about that. Her brother, Edd Clark, was a running back for the Appalachia High School Bulldogs in the late 1960s and was known as the "Stonega Stallion," named after a nearby coal camp where she and he were raised.

Edd set the high school state record for total rushing yards at 5908, scored a career 566 points, and ran the most yards rushed in a single game, 449, only to have the latter record surpassed by his nephew, Thomas Jones, with 462 yards. Jones played football at Powell Valley High School, only two miles away from Appalachia High School. When calculating career yardage and scores, one should keep in mind that until the early 1970s there were no state playoffs in Virginia where stats could pile up for the smaller schools. Edd struggled academically at Purdue and did not penetrate the NFL like his two nephews, Thomas and Julius. Nonetheless, their locally famous uncle was much of a hero. He drowned in Florida while saving children caught in an ocean undertow. Exhausted, he attempted to save another child and died trying. The Stonega Stallion will never be forgotten in the Virginia coalfields.

Edd Clark

And, most recently, Gate City's Mac McClung won the NBA's 2023 dunking competition with a nearly perfect score. At six feet and two inches in height, Mac put on a spectacular feat by showcasing Southwest Virginia's heart and his competitiveness. Then, for good measure, he won the 2024 title with a do-or-die stunning reverse dunk over the head of seven-foot-tall Shaquille O'Neal.

The photos below are courtesy of Mac McClung's many fans.

A perfect dunk

Wearing the Gate City jersey

The History and Culture of Coalfields Southwest Virginia

Pure Excellence

YEARS PRIOR, a dynamic young man wowed his packed high school gym at Castlewood with 100-plus dunks, speed, and grace. Calvin Talford from Dante, a coal town in Russell County, went on to win the NCAA dunking contest. During high school, he set track and field records, and along with two points from one other teammate, won the state championship. What are the odds that two of our coal region's neighboring counties would produce these determined young athletes that excelled in this acrobatic specialty? Maybe I'm too proud of our coalfield achievements to be objective, but there is a pattern to these Virginia coalfield achievements in politics, war, academics and sports. Not too bad for a roughly 3,000 square mile region that is populated by only 200,000 citizens, give or take.

Calvin flying to the rim

CHAPTER 6
OUR YOUNG PEOPLE ARE SMART AND COMPETITIVE, SO WHERE ARE THE GOOD JOBS?

So if our mountain kids are so smart and competitive, why are state and federal agencies and the high-tech private sectors not rushing here to recruit, train, and employ them at great savings in salaries, and with more favorable attrition rates? That is a good question, and millions of public dollars have been spent on studying similar questions regarding impoverished areas of our nation.

As a result of stereotyping, prejudice, and lack of good jobs and hope, a majority of our brainiest leave in bunches each May with high school diplomas in hand to seek careers elsewhere. Once there, they create jobs, enhance their adopted communities, and become productive political and civic leaders in distant places, while we suffer from a shortage of those qualities and human assets. Not all, but many of these bright, energetic young natives would stay, or come back home after learning their crafts. But that retention of tomorrow's Appalachian leaders can happen only if we have the appropriate jobs and opportunities to offer.

Simply put, a modern society cannot survive—much less prosper—when today's best and brightest young talent and tomorrow's potential leaders leave their homes and communities. So yes, negative stereotypes hurt in real ways and we mountain people sure could use an Appalachian anti-defamation league. Maybe some purpose-driven young mountain savants will study this writing and lead the charge. Otherwise, we are on the bumpy road of no return.

But, some skeptical readers might say, this is all in the past and the friendly culture of the coalfields is no more. Let's review a more recent example that such traits still exist when it comes to welcoming strangers and respecting other ideas and religions.

Buchanan County's Appalachian College of Pharmacy, which I founded, very much needed a pharmaceutics professor so the school could attain full accreditation. The problem was that the pharmaceutical industry at that time hired every PhD in the field that they could find. We were in trouble. Fortunately, a highly qualified immigrant from Bangladesh responded to our ad. We promptly fired a male administrator, also an immigrant, for failing to hire this well-qualified applicant because of her religion. Upon learning about this despicable slight, the school gave her an appropriate interview and evaluation that I conducted.

Dr. Masuda then became one of our hardest-working and most-dedicated employees at the school. She, her husband Sham, and their two brilliant daughters were respected and helped by any and all mountain natives they came to know. We found them housing, lean goats, and a mosque, and quickly became their travel guides, friends, and colleagues. In turn, they invited our multicultural science faculty and other lucky guests to their home and laid out a feast of curried meats, delicious vegetables, and incredible desserts.

Try being asked to say grace over a meal hosted by a Muslim family whose guests include Jewish professors, Seventh Day Adventists, Hindus, Baptists, agnostics, and atheists!

Trying not to offend anyone, I sputtered like the Rain Man until rescued by my wife, a seasoned grace whisperer. This is the same Muslim family that graciously forgave me for inadvertently introducing them to pork because I forgot that the Appalachian feast I fed them in return had fatback meat in the pinto beans.

I could not have been prouder when this Muslim wife and husband team interviewed with the *Richmond Times Dispatch*, and declared that of all the places they had lived—including Saudi Arabia, Canada, Texas, Utah, and Florida—they felt most welcomed in the

Virginia coalfields. After they eventually moved away to Richmond, I visited them again as newly sworn U.S. citizens. They warmly reiterated their desire to come back "home" to Appalachia. I hope they do.

Proud U.S. Citizens, Shams Rahman and Dr. Quamrun Masuda, presenting a bountiful South Asian meal, topped off with American apple pie.

And speaking of Buchanan County, likely the most maligned Virginia coalfield county due to its remoteness and being squeezed between the coalfield states of Kentucky and West Virginia, there is a wondrous story of inclusion to tell.

In 1921, a Buchanan County orphan, Sam Hurley, decided to help other at-risk children by founding Mountain Mission School within the town limits of Grundy. Thousands of impoverished (and sometimes abused) mountain kids received housing, education, and inspiration from this faith-based safe place over the decades. As more and more social programs became federally funded in Appalachia, the need for private endemic orphanages waned.

The school had a choice of closing down or reaching out to other desperate children. Hence, the majority of its impoverished students have more recently originated from approximately sixty nations, including many locales in Africa, and Central and South America. A few local children are also enrolled as residents or day students. In fact, the school has the state's top private- and public-school diversity rate of eighty-two percent amongst a pre-COVID student body of 260. Its choir is world-renowned, and the college placement rate is routinely over ninety percent.

Mountain Mission Choir

Mountain Mission School as NACA 2022 National Champions in Division IV Girls Basketball

Appalachian orphans at Mountain Mission School, 1950s

The History and Culture of Coalfields Southwest Virginia

Sam Hurley at the groundbreaking for Mountain Mission School

Mountain Mission student, a future herpetologist, 1940s

To ensure the 100-year-old school's sustainability, two big-name golf tournaments hosted by Jim McGlothlin, a Buchanan County native and former coal operator, raised more than $70 million. Plus, Mountain Mission graduates who aspire to attend college matriculate at some of the best universities in the nation. They do so debt-free, or nearly so, because of Jim, his wife Fran, and many other dedicated benefactors.

Like most Appalachians, Jim was taught by his parents, Woodrow and Sally, to help people in need, particularly children and the elderly, and to be gracious to strangers and the people around him, regardless of income, creed, or race. This nurturing culture is the very good side of coalfield Appalachia.

CHAPTER 7
COALFIELD VIRGINIA'S MILITARY PARTICIPATION AND STANDOUTS

I PREVIOUSLY NOTED that Appalachians are patriots to a fault. This accolade is borne out by the following *Baltimore Sun* article reprinted in memory of the author, Alice Cornett, a prolific and well-respected writer of Appalachia.

The Sgt. York Syndrome
by Alice Cornett
November 11, 1991 | London, Kentucky
London, Kentucky — When U.S. casualty figures in the Persian Gulf War are analyzed, we may learn that this war ended not only the "Vietnam Syndrome," as President Bush proclaimed, but also the so-called "Sergeant York Syndrome," the disproportionate number of casualties among servicemen from Appalachia.

As a percent of its population, the Appalachian region has sustained higher losses in our wars of the past 50 years than has any other section of the country. West Virginia, the only state designated as wholly in Appalachia, had the highest casualty ratio in both World War II and the Vietnam conflict.

In Vietnam, West Virginians died in combat at a rate of 84.1 for every 100,000 of the state's male residents. The national average was 58.9 deaths per 100,000 males.

Parts of 13 other states are classed as Appalachian counties, and these outdistanced the non-Appalachian counties in Vietnam casualties. Kentucky's Appalachian counties averaged 84.2 deaths per 100,000 males; the rest of Kentucky averaged 64.4.

Ohio, generally perceived as a Midwestern state, has a few Appalachian counties along its borders with West Virginia and Kentucky. These averaged 78.4 losses in Vietnam per 100,000 males while for the rest of Ohio, the figure was 59.5.

Theories put forward to explain this startling disparity have focused on the character and the military heritage of residents of Appalachia as well as the region's perennially poor economy. Unshakable patriotism and a willingness to fight for his country have long been attributes of the Southern mountaineer.

That tradition goes back to the Revolutionary War Battle of Kings Mountain where backwoodsmen from western Virginia, the Carolinas, and Georgia sent the British trained Tories packing.

Breathitt County in Eastern Kentucky won distinction during World War I as the only county in America without a single draftee. Its military quota was readily filled by enlistments. Poverty cannot be overlooked, however, as an impetus to military service. With limited access to higher education, and never enough jobs to go around, many Appalachians have found few alternatives to military service. The probability of being killed in war seemed scarcely greater than that of being killed in a coal mine.

In a 1976 *Washington Monthly* article, James Fallows called Vietnam "the class war," pointing out that although Selective Service was in effect, Vietnam was our first war in which all segments of American society did not participate equally. The wealthier and better educated remained in college, sought other legal loopholes to the draft, or left the country. Those who did the fighting, Mr. Fallows wrote, came by and large from the under classes—Appalachians, Blacks from the inner cities and the South, and Hispanics from the barrios.

While this argument would seem to have validity, it does not account for unequal losses based on a purely geographical standpoint. Statistics make clear that an Appalachian's chance of dying in battle for his country has been significantly greater than that risk has been for other Americans. It appears that certain characteristics—including a particular aptness for combat—have made him a prime target.

"Appalachians make good soldiers, and the Army knows it," said Steven Giles, chief psychologist at the Mountain Home, Tenn., Veterans Administration Medical Center. Dr. Giles, who compiled a study of U.S. war casualties, is credited with coining the term "Sergeant York Syndrome." Sgt. Alvin York was the Tennessee mountain man who single-handedly captured 90 German soldiers in the Argonne in 1918 and received the Medal of Honor. York had been a conscientious objector to the draft, but was persuaded that military service was not incompatible with his beliefs.

Although they serve in all branches of the armed forces, Appalachians are especially valued by the Army. As recruits, they arrive already familiar with the rifle, the infantryman's weapon, and with knowledge of rough terrain. Officers interviewed by Dr. Giles told him that men from Appalachia were preferred for patrols, or to "walk point"—leading the platoon into unknown territory.

Nine percent of U.S. military forces in the Korean War were from areas of Appalachia, but 18 percent of the Medals of Honor awarded in that war went to Appalachians. In Vietnam, they made up 8 percent of our troops and received 13 percent of the Medals of Honor.

In the Persian Gulf War, U.S. fighting tactics changed dramatically. The emphasis shifted from the foot soldier to sophisticated weapons systems delivered by aircraft or launched from remote sites. The new combat style appears to hold a promise that the unequal losses in past conflicts may never be repeated. In fact, our casualties in Desert Storm were so light that, for statistical purposes, they may be inconclusive—and it is too soon to say whether the Sergeant York Syndrome still operates. Perhaps it will not outlast this century, or this generation.

[end of article]

While many, many Appalachian warriors have received the Medal of Honor and other citations for valor in combat, two of them stand out. Sergeant Alvin York, mentioned by Cornett, is buried in his coalfield county of Fentress, Tennessee. His faith, grace, combat readiness, skill, and tactics during World War I are well-documented and showcased by Hollywood.

Closer to my childhood home, five miles to be exact, a rambunctious young man from Castlewood, Virginia, became the unofficial Sergeant York of World War II.

Junior James Spurrier (born James Ira Spurrier) was a U.S. Army soldier who received the military's two highest decorations for valor: the Medal of Honor and the Distinguished Service Cross. He also received the Croix de Guerre from France and a like medal from Belgium. Overall, he received seventeen military medals during his WWII stint.

Junior dropped out of Russell County's school system in the sixth grade to help his family during the Great Depression. When his mother died, he joined the Civilian Conservation Corps in West Virginia to send money back home, like many young people did during that time of nationwide poverty. Soon thereafter, Uncle Sam had other plans for these work-hardened young men, so Junior came back home to Southwest Virginia, then enlisted in the U.S. Army at a faraway Richmond induction center.

He first fought in the Pacific Theater, and after being seriously wounded came back to the states for medical care. When deemed fit to return to service he requested to go back to the battlefield. He was assigned to the 35th Infantry Division and shipped out to Europe after the D-Day invasion.

On September 16, 1944, near Lay-Saint-Christophe, France, Junior personally assaulted a hill where German defenders were dug in and raining hot lead and mortar shells upon the American soldiers below. After his unit took cover, Junior manned an abandoned machine gun and in short order killed over a dozen Nazis and forced the surrender of twenty-two more. Running out of ammo, he, through stealth and determination, circled behind the enemy's active machine gun nests and hurled hand grenades that sent many more Nazis to Hades, much to the delight of his pinned-down buddies. The estimated German fatalities imposed by this single fighter ranged in the dozens (counting bodies while chasing the fleeing Nazis was not a priority as U.S. soldiers pressed Hitler's forces out of France and into their native country for the ultimate coup-de-grace). Obviously, Junior favored up-close-and-personal valor.

Then on November 13, 1944, this mountain Rambo single-handedly attacked dug-in German forces in Achain, France. By that time, this very independent twenty-two-year-old scrapper had a reputation amongst his officers and fellow soldiers for deciding on his own how best to annihilate the enemy. While his fellow soldiers waited for the command to attack, Junior slipped around to the rear of the town and started waylaying Germans, alone. A reporter for *American Legion Magazine* who was familiar with Junior concluded that after swiping a can of peaches from the mess sergeant and feeling very frisky, he jumped the orderly lineup "secretly hoping there were enough Germans in the place to give him a fight."

Hearing the premature noise of machine guns, rifles, grenades, and at least one bazooka, the commanding officer, Colonel Roecker, inquired by walkie-talkie what had happened. His combat officer reluctantly speculated that Junior must have been impatient and started the battle without them. The Colonel then gave this epic order: "Attack Achain! Company G from the east and Spurrier from the west!"

The rest of the main unit attacked as directed and was promptly pinned down by blazing machine gun fire. With very little combat help, Spurrier liberated the entire occupied town that day after hours of hide-and-seek tactics. He used a Browning Automatic Rifle, his M1 rifle, a captured bazooka, various pistols, plus American and German hand grenades, all while under intense fire.

Some of the surviving Nazis sought refuge in a barn filled with hay and barrels of fuel. Like any clever country boy would have done, Junior set this very volatile mix on fire! He then captured numerous soldiers as they ran from the inferno. As Hollywood might have scripted, he ended his assault astride a "borrowed" German motorcycle. As he sped through the corpse-littered village streets, Junior clipped another enemy soldier or two with pistols blazing. During these several hours of combat he killed a German officer and twenty-five enlisted soldiers, captured two more officers, and nabbed a dozen more erstwhile Aryan supermen.

His final estimated kill and capture counts of the two battles combined: 40-50 dead and 36 captured Nazis; Hitler, 0.

Not to be overly morbid, but even Junior did not know how many of the enemy he took out. After he passed away, a fellow soldier contacted his nephew and stated that our mountain gladiator saved many unknown lives of his fellow soldiers and French citizens. Evidently when Junior was in a bad mood or bored, he would leave his sentry post at night, sneak across the enemy lines, and pick off unsuspecting enemy guards and scouts. After one of these unauthorized forays, Uncle Junior came back to his unit, and as he took off his military jacket, two loose German bullets fell out of the shot-up garment and hit the ground. Junior, nonplussed, was quoted to have said, "they are getting better," and walked off.

Junior received the nickname "Task Force Spurrier" from his unit. He earned it.

After returning home, he pitched for a minor league baseball team in Galax, Virginia, and with a 1-1 record he decided he was a better soldier than baseball player. He re-enlisted in the Army in 1947, and eventually found himself in Korea.

Due to what we now know as PTSD symptoms, made worse by alcohol, he was routinely disciplined, and in 1951 received a general discharge. Back in the States, Junior was easily agitated and got involved in more than one barroom brawl. I can only imagine what happened when some tanked-up honkytonk bully challenged Junior to step outside to fight!

After his last brush with the law, Junior stopped drinking and became a radio and TV repairman. This mostly unheralded American hero lived in a Tennessee cabin until his death in 1984. This sad ending takes nothing away from his undaunted courage and love of country. Junior's battlefield exploits were captured by this Army illustration.

The History and Culture of Coalfields Southwest Virginia

Credit: Yank Magazine

A painting of the likeness of Staff Sgt. J. I. "Junior" Spurrier receiving his medal of honor from General Dwight Eisenhower in February of 1945 hangs in the Mercer County's "Those Who Served" War Museum in Princeton, West Virginia.

MEDAL OF HONOR
SSG JUNIOR J. SPURRIER
WORLD WAR II | 13 NOVEMBER 1944

STAFF SGT. JUNIOR J. SPURRIER

Back Home in Coalfield Appalachia

Most recently, Junior has been honored with a resolution from the Virginia General Assembly and a wall of honor with beautiful plaques, pictures, and replicas of his many medals, including the Medal of Honor, located at the author's St. Paul law office building in 2023.

Junior's plaques, replica medals, and images are one of three veteran memorial sites in St. Paul. UVA-Wise student, Suzanne Scheerer, gave guests a tour of the regional museum in the same building.

Russell County supervisor Lou Ann Wallace represents Junior's Castlewood District homeplace and emceed the celebration of his new memorial wall attached to the author's law office building in St. Paul.

Keynote speaker Lt. Governor Winsome Earles-Sears, a Marine veteran, being photographed by Del. Terry Kilgore and introduced by Sen. Todd Pillion (sitting next to the flag), an Iraq War veteran.

The Lt. Governor in a priceless hug with Junior's cousin, who attended the event along with a large crowd of patriots.

PS: By the way, when is a movie about this unsung hero going to be produced? Someone with connections please call Brad Pitt, Clint Eastwood, or Rambo. They won't get back to me, must be my dialect.

The History and Culture of Coalfields Southwest Virginia

Shifty Powers

If you have seen the *Band of Brothers* series you will recall Shifty Powers, the coolest sharpshooter in the outfit. He was raised in Clinchco, Virginia, a small coal town located in Dickenson County. Residing across Hazel Mountain about twenty-five miles from my boyhood home, he got his nickname for shifty basketball moves.

Like all Appalachian boys of that era, he was taught at a very young age how to effectively use firearms and stealth while hunting squirrels, grouse, ground hogs, and such. Larger animals—deer and turkey, for example—were very scarce in the coalfields when WWII broke out. Mountain families struggling to live day-to-day during the Great Depression cleared out most of the wild game, and only within recent decades have deer, turkey, bear, and bobcats made a big comeback.

Shifty was the man the field commanders called upon when a long shot at a distant Nazi sniper or forward scout was in order. Evidently, he perfected the head-shot-under-pressure and did his part to end the war. Like my WWII dad, he hated Nazis until the day he passed!

Shifty Powers, a true patriot.

CHAPTER 8
COAL MINING

OF COURSE, like many communities worldwide, especially where poverty reigns, Appalachia has a dark side and those negative images always seem to "hawg" the headlines. We are easy targets because we rarely fight back. Fortunately, this *laissez faire* attitude seems to be changing.

But first know that most readers of this book will likely be surprised to learn that many of our fifty states have mined coal at some point in their histories. As mentioned, the first commercially mined coal by Europeans and their descendants occurred near Richmond, Virginia, in 1701. The first Native Americans to use coal are believed to be the Hopi tribe in the 1300s. Even Hawaii had small deposits of the black stuff in collapsed volcanoes that filled with rotted vegetation over the years before forming into peat, then sub-bituminous coal.

The following map sets out the nation's areas of coal deposits ranging from anthracite, bituminous, sub-bituminous, and lignite, listed in order of purity.

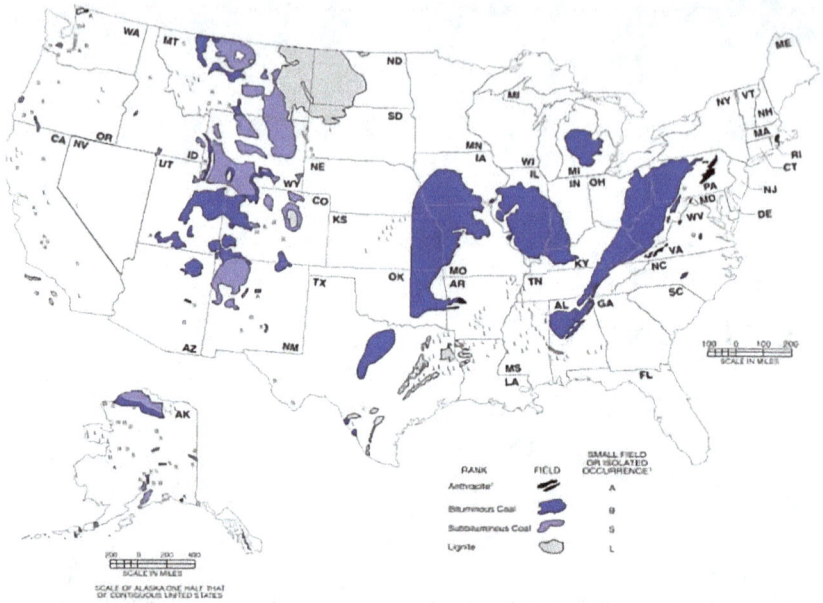

The states of West Virginia, Pennsylvania, and Kentucky have always been on the top production list for Appalachian coal, some of the purest in the world. Outside of Appalachia, Wyoming currently produces the most coal of any state in the nation by far; yet its BTU (British Thermal Unit) quality is far less than the more ancient coal in our hills.

Coal production in the Appalachian states has plummeted during the past decades, particularly the past several years. As steam-coal demand dries up due to power plants switching to cheap (and less polluting) natural gas and renewable sources, the only secure source of coal jobs emanates from the mining of metallurgical coal used for steel production.

Appalachia still hosts a substantial supply of high-grade "met" coal seams and, unless a substitute for coking coal is developed, the only coal mining jobs in Appalachia will eventually be of that variety. Metallurgical coal seams, such as the Pocahontas seams, that run through parts of southwest Virginia and southern West Virginia, have a BTU content of 15,000 or so (triple that of Wyoming coal). This Appalachian "rocket fuel coal" burns so clean that it is referred to as "smokeless." Much like anthracite coal located farther east in the Appalachians, the purity of bituminous coal depends upon geological pressure, the age of the coal's formation, and how the great swamps that produced the peat moss (that turned into coal) were mixed and matched with sand, mud, and trace minerals.

While many coal-mining advocates tend to blame the EPA for coal's decline, there are many factors at play. The EPA, in reality, does not have primary oversight of coal-mining-related environmental issues. Those regulatory enforcements rest on the federal level with the U.S. Office of Surface Mining (OSM) and myriad state agencies that have primacy as long as they follow federal guidelines set forth by Congress in what is usually referred to as the Surface Mining Act of 1977.

The overall decline of eastern coal was already in progress when tighter enforcement of existing laws was vigorously applied under the Obama administration. Federal courts also gave opponents of mountaintop removal operations an edge for the first time through stricter interpretations of permanent streams and other hydrological issues. The following map is useful in tracking coal deposits and poverty in Appalachia.

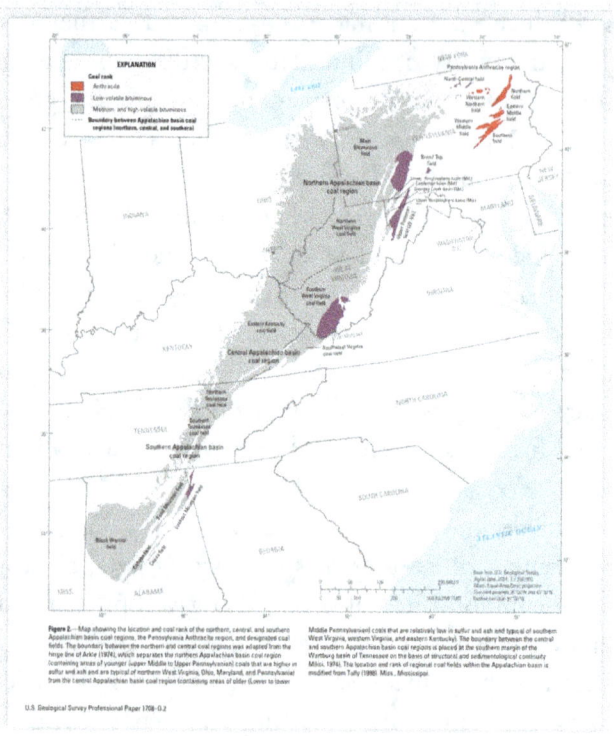

Coal deposits throughout Appalachia

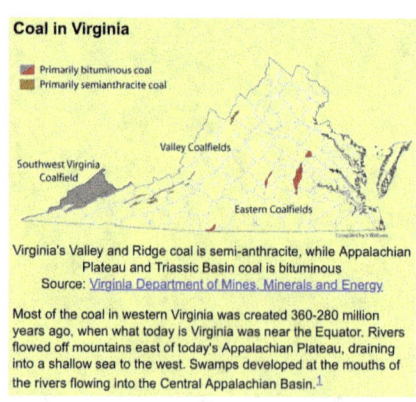

Coal deposits in Virginia

It is easy to conclude when mining joblessness rates are mentioned on TV or the Internet that laid-off miners can simply switch to other good-paying middle-class jobs. Not so; such occupations are rarely available in the actual coalfields.

Mining and related occupations were the dominant employers in the region for well over a century. Therefore, other potential industries did not locate in the coalfields because of intermittent labor shortages during coal-mining economic booms and potential unionization efforts. Unionization is no longer a factor, but good work ethics are still alive and well.

Another reason well-meaning investors do not target the actual Appalachian coalfield region proper (where poverty and runaway depopulations are most active) is that many of them are geographically misinformed.

For example, when the word "coalfields" is mentioned in the more prosperous venues in Virginia, it is assumed by many job creators that every county west of Roanoke or Wytheville is in that column. The City of Roanoke is 162 miles east of the town of St. Paul, the nearest gateway to the coalfields that lie west of the Clinch River.

Obviously non-coalfield Appalachia in general, and coalfield Appalachia specifically, have a geographical communications problem, added to a long list of other misconceptions. The best rule of thumb when it comes to Virginia is if you are not west of the Clinch River, you are not in the actual coal-producing coalfields. Following that path westward, one soon arrives in neighboring eastern Kentucky. A huge 10,500 square miles of actual coal counties are ensconced in the Appalachian region of the Bluegrass State. It's a geology thing: no coal, no actual coalfields.

To put a face on unemployed miners, *America Al Jazeera* published a February 2016, article detailing the number of Black families impacted by out-migration caused by the disappearance of this traditional pathway to the middle class.

Coal mining literally offered people of all walks of life a fighting chance to reach the American Dream, regardless of educational degrees or race. That opportunity was especially important to impoverished Black Americans, immigrants, and dirt-poor multi-generational

Appalachians. The following statistics in the *Al Jazeera* article starkly sum up a dying middle class in the coalfields:

"In the 1930s, coal employed 55,000 black miners. In 2014, the most recent year for which Bureau of Labor Statistics data are available, only about 2,500 black people worked as coal miners — fewer than 3 percent of the total." (written by Roger May for *Al Jazeera America*)

According to this well-written piece, the average yearly income of a Black family in 1929 was $420, while a Black miner could earn $1,400. That upward disparity of higher incomes helps explain the reluctance to leave a place known as home, but there is more to that feeling as set forth by the article's author: "Still, (Black) families who've lived here for generations say they're reluctant to leave. They praise the region's physical beauty, close-knit family life and friendly Southern manners."

CHAPTER 9
THE UNITED MINE WORKERS OF AMERICA

PREFACE: *The nation's largest violent domestic uprising since the Civil War occurred in neighboring West Virginia more than a hundred years ago. This several- day confrontation between poorly treated coal miners, many of whom were WWI veterans, and very well-connected coal company owners and their private security forces made daily national headlines. Thousands of armed miners confronted the dug-in coal company guards and public police forces in reaction to a coal-company-arranged assassination of the little town of Matewan's very popular pro-union chief of police, Sid Hatfield. Sid previously had a showdown in his town with company detectives that resulted in the killing of several of them, including two siblings of the owner of the security company, Baldwin-Felts.*

This deadly retaliation became so violent that the United Mine Workers of America withdrew its support and even Mother Jones, a hugely popular pro-miner figurehead, publicly called for a cease fire to no avail. Only the U.S. Army could settle down the feud after attacking the miners and issuing a threat of full-out suppression.

Both the miners and the coal company's private army were in violation of the concepts of justice and due process. Nonetheless, incremental improvement of mine safety and decent wages emerged due to public sentiment for the mistreated workers and the extreme overreach of some of the coal company owners and the politicians that supported them.

THESE TYPES of labor violence permeated the Appalachian coalfields as aggrieved miners took great umbrage that safety was an afterthought, and that job security was non-existent. Conditions improved only after the United Mine Workers of America (UMWA) teamed up with other labor organizations to demand that states and the federal government take action. This standoff went on for more than a century, and today the union is struggling to survive while still pushing for pension and healthcare protection, plus pro-labor legislation.

One of the causes of the union's steady decline of political power and influence emanated from "wildcat strikes," so named because union employees would sometimes leave the workplace without UMWA authorization. The only requirement for such a walk-off to occur was the demand of one or more individual miners. Many times, these non-sanctioned strikes would shut down all coal production for that particular company.

Occasionally these AWOL actions spread to other coal companies that had no hand in whatever the original grievance was about. This behavior caused substantial economic losses and breaches of contract with coal-hungry industrial customers, including power plants and steel mills. At times the instigators of the strike would not, or could not, clearly state a valid grievance as union leaders attempted to get them back to work to avoid violations of the UMWA's contract with the Bituminous Coal Operators Association (BCOA).

When UMWA members took on the mantra "all for one and one for all" well over a century ago, they literally meant it. The more-seasoned coal miners of that era, who had lived through the Great Depression, a devastating world war, and multiple coal strikes, were legitimately worried that such rash walkouts would have permanent and devastating consequences.

My dad, Arthur Kilgore, his rowdy brother Harmon, and their workaholic cousin Clinton many times would report to work at the Moss 2 Clinchfield Coal Company mines just to turn around and come back home because one (usually younger) miner decided he didn't want to work that night. Their late-night-early-morning work period was locally known as the "hoot owl shift," and so it was particularly frustrating to drive back home at 1 a.m., empty handed, with nowhere to go and nothing constructive to do.

Instead of calling in sick, the disgruntled employee or employees would cause their union brothers (and sisters) and the company to lose millions in wages and profits. The elder miners' fear of retaliation against unjustified walkouts became a reality when in 1989, the union's last "big strike" was a do-or-die event for all parties. In a way, it seemed that Pittston Coal Company drew the short straw among unionized coal companies to have a showdown with the UMWA. Economically speaking, the company's goal was to either sink or swim. The Pittston coal strike brought the wildcat problem and other festering issues to a head in the coalfields of Virginia, with nationwide labor ramifications.

However, wildcatting was only part of the dispute, as coal companies realized that pension funds and healthcare costs were mounting and that every bad business decision they made put them deeper in hock. Neither side "won," as Pittston eventually sold its properties and liabilities to non-union companies, most of which eventually went bankrupt.

By that time, many non-union operations were led by a new generation of less confrontational and more cerebral mine owners who took safety more seriously and paid their miners the same, if not more, than the union scale. All of these factors, plus the increase in automation and a steady drop in demand for coal, leaves the UMWA of today with relatively few members who are actively mining coal. Nonetheless, the United Mine Workers of America's legacy will always be strongly tied to coal and Appalachia.

My law firm represented almost every union miner and their supporters arrested during the Pittston strike. This protest movement (that started out peacefully, as most do) generated thousands of court cases, most of which were for non-violent misdemeanors. Violent and non-violent felony charges made up about ten percent of arrests.

Although that year-plus-long struggle deserves a book of its own regarding its judicial aspects, it is only fair to point out that the UMWA, for the first time that I know of in its history, allowed its members to work without a contract in a vain attempt to avoid a strike.

Pittston, which had withdrawn from the BCOA shortly before its decision to go non-union, made no concessions and ultimately took away health coverage support for retirees and demanded mandatory overtime and working on Sundays. It seemed, at least to mining families, that the company took these unprecedented measures just to provoke a strike.

When company support for "widows and orphans" funds was suspended during the fourteen months of working without a contract, the 1,800 Pittston miners were finally authorized by their union to strike. Soon thereafter, 30,000 of the union's 80,000 nationwide active members walked off the job in support of the Virginia miners who were being used as a test to see if the fabled UMWA could finally be minimized or outright destroyed.

Three lawyer associates, multiple legal assistants, our office manager (my big sister Jean), and I worked around the clock to keep up with the resulting flood of state court labor-related criminal proceedings in eight counties, as well as numerous related hearings in federal court.

Huge rallies of miners and their supporters generated large donations in support for the UMWA strike fund managed by a non-profit entity. When Pittston changed from union to non-union, their facilities were primed for a union shutdown. The union designated key company operations to be shut down. Hundreds, and sometimes thousands, of miners and supporters would block the entrances to what were called "scabs," which was also the name for non-union workers that replaced the UMWA members.

Some highlights are worth mentioning, since I lived this strike well after it ended because our pending court cases still went forward to conclusion. In what may be a national record, my associate, Scott Mullins, and I caused 428 misdemeanor cases to be dismissed after a one-hour hearing. Our clients and supporters packed the court room and hallways of the Russell County, Virginia, courthouse, and the milling and passionate defendants not able to find room inside stretched up and down the steep back street. Everyone—except lawyers, judges, and bailiffs—wore camouflage T-shirts, pants, and jackets adorned with strike emblems and epitaphs, some of which were salty for that era.

These particular defendants had participated in a sit-down (and lay-down) strike at the entrance of a huge coal preparation facility called Moss 3 Prep Plant. When built in the 1950s, this technical wonder was the largest coal processing facility in the world.

The Virginia State Police and a variety of federal agencies brought in dozens of extra officers to carry out the various court orders mandating that the strikers obey the law. On this special sit-in day, the state police, the majority of whom treated the strikers and sympathizers with respect, had to carry 428 men and women, large and small, onto buses to have them processed several miles away at a youth detention center in the same county.

After the duly elected prosecutor in a very busy coal county was removed because he was a partner in a coal company that mined Pittston coal, a special prosecutor was assigned to take his place. Unfortunately for the substitute lawyer, the officers who saw the protestors block the entrances were busy loading them onto buses while other officers at a distant detention center formally placed them under arrest.

Under Virginia law, misdemeanor convictions require that the complaining witness have direct knowledge of the offense, usually by personally seeing the infraction occur. Of course, other methods of prosecution are allowed, including confessions. What is *not* allowed is for the officer who saw the incident to hand over the alleged perpetrator to an arresting officer who did not witness the infraction. As for confessions, not one of our 1,400 or so clients (many had multiple charges) ever talked with state or federal authorities, much less confessed. This may also be a national record for non-squealing.

We suggested to the judge that if the special prosecutor agreed with our logic, then he could put on his best case against a single defendant; however, if he lost that argument, all 428 cases would be dismissed. Conversely, if he prevailed, all of our clients would be found guilty without further hearings if the judge so ruled. Otherwise, we would have tried the cases one at a time which would have taken several weeks, if not months. Despite the various ethical and technical issues this proposal created, we were fairly sure we would prevail.

The new prosecutor readily agreed, and when we cross-examined his token arresting officer and asked him if he saw the token defendant break the law, he had to admit that he and his cohorts were nowhere near the scene of the alleged crime.

Bang!

All of the cases were summarily dismissed and the word spread quickly up and down the hallways and out into the back street. Yelling and whooping ensued as we left the courtroom; back slapping, congratulatory hooting, and macho compliments came from every direction, not exactly what trial lawyers are used to encountering.

To our chagrin, the special prosecutor endured some very graphic suggestions, some of which were anatomically impossible to execute, as he tried to walk through the gauntlet of revved-up miners and supporters lining the hallways and backstreet where he had unwittingly parked his car.

I went back to rescue Bob and walked him to his car. Whenever some of my clients would loudly protest that I was "on the other side," I would mention that the prosecutor was a U.S. Marine and Vietnam War vet. The crowd parted like the Red Sea and many of them, especially the war veterans, shook Bob's hand on his slow way out.

The History and Culture of Coalfields Southwest Virginia

Virginia State Police arresting coal miners who were blocking a road to a coal preparation plant

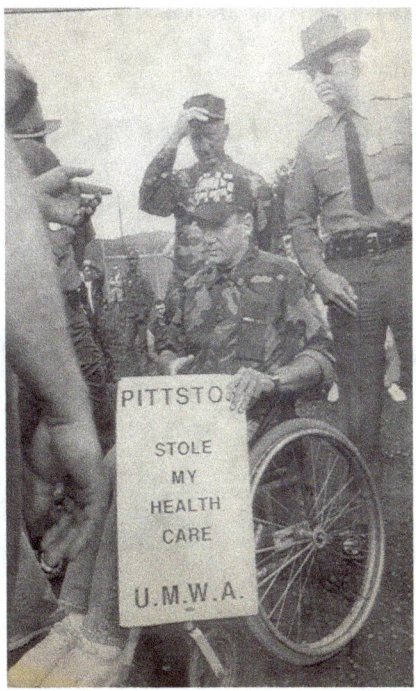

Gail Gentry, Wise, Virginia, a victim of a coal mining accident

Prayer at a Russell County UMWA rally

Women miners and supporters during a "sit down" strike,
similar to earlier civil rights movements

I had a few close calls of being arrested myself, which would have been a cred-builder among my clients but not so much with the Virginia State Bar.

Soon thereafter, I was in the same circuit court awaiting the "true bills" (indictments) issued by the grand jury against several of my clients. The judge solemnly read off the true bills against the suspects who were indicted to stand trial. He then looked at me with a sly grin as he read the last one: "Not a true bill for Frank Kilgore." I did not realize that I was on the menu.

I was a little stunned, and somewhat disgruntled, that the substitute prosecutor thought I needed to be jailed for performing my mandatory duty of informing my clients about the Fifth Amendment of the United States Constitution. But my newly indicted clients thought it was very cool that I was unknowingly before the same grand jury as they were and had the skills to avoid their fate. I mentioned that jury nullification was likely working its magic, but they were not having any of that excuse.

I should have basked in the moment, not downplayed it. I guess I was just being demure as I imagined being led out of the courtroom in cuffs while my fellow lawyers made bets on my fate.

The second time I thought I might be arrested was when a UMWA strike coordinator called with a hypothetical question, or so he claimed. He asked (hypothetically) that if a union wanted to take over, for instance, a soup factory in protest of the company's bad treatment of its employees, what would be the best way to avoid as many criminal charges as possible for doing so?

Still thinking he was joking, I went along with this "what-if" discussion and asked him if the company was publicly traded on the stock exchange, and he said, "yes, hypothetically." So I opined that the union members wanting to take over the soup plant should buy ten shares each of the company stock, storm in and declare a minority stockholders' meeting, and then invite the soup company officers and other stockholders to participate. I promptly forgot the silly conversation; he did not.

Two weeks later, ninety-nine of my clients, all wearing camouflaged clothes and sporting backpacks filled with food, water, and underwear (and possibly Jack Daniels), rushed the coal company's largest coal preparation plant with the Stars and Stripes waving. This headlong entourage of shouting miners ran off the replacement workers and company security guards in one fell swoop. Each one of the invaders had exactly ten shares of Pittston stock in their pockets.

This takeover made international news, and sure enough, the newly minted minority stockholders called a corporate meeting to be conducted at the prep plant. The technical problem was that no outsider stockholder or company official could attend because thousands of striking miners from across Appalachia and their nationwide supporters had the public road blocked for days. After a week or so, I was directed by a federal judge and the UMWA vice-president to go retrieve my clients from the occupied prep plant. The point had been made.

I cannot fathom the number of charges that would have been placed against me, including accessory before, during, and after the fact, if the union coordinator had not explained the actual circumstances to the media. Thankfully, he also disclosed to the authorities that he checked with a lawyer first, without mentioning my name, but that he had made a joke of his hypothetical and then he and the lawyer laughed it off. I was not laughing the day of the takeover.

Below are a few of my prep plant buddies, many of whom are Vietnam War vets along with one or two Korean War elders.

Courtesy of Earl Dotter

The History and Culture of Coalfields Southwest Virginia

Courtesy of Earl Dotter

Courtesy of Earl Dotter

At the time of this all-consuming strike, I had no idea that thirty-some years later I would be promoting the same 1,800 acre parcel for job-creating industrial development. The shuttered prep plant has been removed, and 230 acres of prime, ready-to-build, heavy industrial sites are there today, replete with two electrical sources, multiple railroad sidings, ample water, natural gas, and access to top-drawer solar and geothermal sites. We humans rarely get to truly live a full-circle journey such as this.

Another curious strike-related story involved our local circuit court judge who presided over the strike-related injunction cases. Almost all of the resident judges in the Virginia coal region declared a conflict of interest because they were either from extended union families or had long-term relations with union members during their law practices.

The only judge that did not recuse himself was the son of a veteran state legislator. The judge's dad was very defiant and colorful at times, and one of the most engaging mountain characters I have ever met. When some union members pressured him to support their cause he refused, citing the illegal activities that were emerging.

His son eventually levied $64 million in fines against the union for violating picket line restrictions and other offenses. These fines were later dismissed by the U.S. Supreme Court upon various legal grounds. Had the fines been imposed, the union would have likely been bankrupted.

The History and Culture of Coalfields Southwest Virginia

Courtesy of Earl Dotter

As a direct result of the local judge's rulings, an unprecedented political movement ensued. His dad, a pugnacious lawyer and two-fisted mountaineer in his own right, came up for re-election during the strike. Being a seasoned incumbent, his tenth or so re-election was a foregone conclusion as his political party was back then locally dominated by coal miner families and union members. They routinely voted as a bloc for the party of Franklin Delano Roosevelt (FDR), a "friend of the working man" and literally the savior and fierce promoter of blue-collar jobs during the Great Depression.

Standing Strong for Jobs. Courtesy of Earl Dotter

As a kid selling door-to-door anything from newspapers and garden seeds to glittered wall-hanger religious mottos, I noticed that almost every coal miner household I visited had these images on their living room walls: John L. Lewis (the intimidating titan leader of the United Mine Workers during its heyday), presidents Franklin D. Roosevelt and John F. Kennedy, and a rendition of Jesus.

That was in the days when the Democratic Party owned the loyalty of Appalachia's rank-and-file workers. This was simply the way things worked politically in coalfield Appalachia as this very confident state legislator, himself a World War II vet, prepared to win reelection unopposed by any challenger on the ballot.

Literally three weeks before the election, Cecil Roberts, the vice-president (now president) of the UMWA, directed a popular union official from the same county as the incumbent to run as a write-in candidate. The designated protest candidate, Jackie Stump, was jailed along with Cecil for violating court orders, serving several days at the beginning of the strike. Jackie received much press coverage for his ensuing prolonged "hunger strike." Jackie, now deceased, was much of a man and we were mystified when he left jail weighing the same, if not more, as the day he was arrested.

In any event, Jackie at first resisted running as a write-in candidate against a local political powerhouse icon. He feared he would be the laughing stock of the coalfield region after he got thrashed at the polls and argued that such a loss would, in turn, weaken the union's cause. That was a very clever theory and revealed Jackie's hard-learned lessons after years of navigating his way through UMWA bare-knuckle politics.

Vice-President Roberts was unmoved; he marshaled all of the strikers receiving the UMWA-funded weekly strike pay of $200 to go door-to-door throughout the legislative district and inform thousands of voters that Jackie would not be on the ballot, "but here is how to write him in."

Union helpers fanned out over every precinct on Election Day to literally show voters how to complete the write-in ballots, which was a much more obscure process in those days than now. That night, Jackie was announced the winner by a 2-to-1 margin.

Everyone assumed he would be a labor firebrand as an Independent and rail against the stubborn remnants of the state legislature's so-called Byrd Machine, which opposed all unions and openly supported segregation not so long prior to this election. Being smart, Jackie caucused with the dominant party and their huge majority. He immediately sponsored common-sense bills that had a chance of passing to help not only his avid coal mining supporters, but also the rest of his constituency that lacked potable water, good roads, and efficient public services. Unfortunately, his predecessor's ongoing successes in those same efforts were soon lost in the passion of a life-and-death strike.

Delegate Jackie Stump with his baby girl, Aubrey, in his Virginia General Assembly office

There are other unlikely election surprises in Virginia during my voting lifetime that compare to Jackie's improbable victory. One is, of course, the election of the nation's first Black governor (in the Cradle of the Confederacy, of all places).

Like any good Hollywood story, these underdogs won and made history. I could go on and on about the Pittston/UMWA battle, but hopefully my law firm's stash of court cases, recollections, and photos from that epic strike will someday be of assistance to a future author.

To be fair, there were coal companies over the decades that strongly supported local civic efforts. They built schools, churches, and hospitals, and provided running water, housing, and entertainment for their employees and families. Miners had to pay for most of the benefits, of course, but the free new schools and churches were invaluable to a very diverse, pro-religion community. Those new schools, along with missionary facilities and faith-based colleges established by Episcopal, Catholic, Methodist, and Baptist organizations, were a lifeline for education in the coalfields.

Moreover, many of the union coal companies went much further than this to provide for their workers and families. As time went on, local owners of non-union mining operations from the mountains helped start and fund many civic, educational, and sports endeavors. Obviously this civic-minded attitude also helped motivate their miners to resist unionization efforts, especially when higher wages and no loss of pay due to strikes took hold.

I know many coal company owners who I tussled with for decades over court cases, red-hot politics, and occasionally on a hostile personal basis. Over time, some of us came together to help our coalfield region on many levels.

For example, Jim McGlothlin, a Buchanan County native and the founder of United Coal Company, has poured millions of dollars into higher education, job creation, and child development programs; additionally, he has helped the entire state advance in art, education, and civic outreach. Jim's boyhood friend Clyde Stacy and Clyde's business partner John Matney stay busy creating job opportunities in our mountain region as well.

Buchanan County natives, including Jim's little brothers Tom and Mickey, are in a position to become number one in philanthropy when compared to the rest of the Virginia coalfields. This fortuitous generational outcome came about because northern speculators did not swoop into that more remote county and take the huge majority of coal and gas wealth back home to city shareholders, as they did in other coal counties. Standard-gauge railroads in that coal- and gas-rich county were not available until the 1930s due to Buchanan County's very steep terrain; that delay was crucial in the accumulation of local coal ownership and wealth.

This opportunity allowed the county's budding local entrepreneurs to figure out that landowners in neighboring coal counties had been hoodwinked into selling their precious commodities for as little as fifty cents an acre. Percentage-wise, many landowners in Buchanan kept their coal intact, which later blossomed into the presence of a generous cadre of benefactors.

Another Buchanan County native, Steve Smith, succeeded his dad Jack in the grocery business. That private chain, Food City, now employs 16,000 workers in Southwest Virginia and Northeast Tennessee (and beyond). Steve and his family step up when it comes to helping their coal and non-coal Appalachian service areas during and after natural disasters. They also supply local school needs, market locally raised meat and vegetables, and bring tens of thousands of tourists into the area during sponsored NASCAR events. Other very helpful foundations that support the county's rebirth include the family of Boyd Fowler, the Baxter Foundation, and the Booth Foundation. This latter foundation, along with the Shott Foundation, Thompson Foundation, and Elgin Foundation, have supported educational and other projects in Buchanan County and Tazewell County as well.

Maybe there is something in the water in Buchanan County that engenders "helping thy neighbor." (Disclosure: I represented Buchanan County as assistant county attorney for thirteen years and we got a lot done, including establishing two graduate schools, the beginning of a flood-proof mega mountain-top development site, and making the county Virginia's Elk Capital!) The motto there is "whatever it takes."

Wise County has its benefactors as well. Carl Smith and his widow Hunter have generously donated funds for academics and sports at the University of Virginia's College at Wise (UVAW). The Richard and Leslie Gilliam Foundation supports many coalfield civic and academic endeavors; Marvin and Marsha Gilliam are robust supporters of higher education as is the Napoleon Hill Foundation. Neighboring Dickenson County has the Columbus Phipps Foundation, which I helped establish, that offers scholarships to county students that wish to attend UVAW. Russell County's Thelma and Robert Hancock Scholarship funds emphasize financial support for needy Southwest Virginia students that attend UVAW, particularly students from Dickenson and Russell counties. As the executor of the Hancock estate, I am thrilled to receive yearly letters from Appalachian students that receive these crucial funds. It is particularly heartwarming to hear from first-generation scholars who have a great motivational impact upon siblings, cousins, and friends.

Another honorable and former coal company owner, Mike Quillen of Gate City, Virginia, serves on college boards and economic development organizations where he supports many civic and community projects. When he received his first five-million-dollar stock dividend from the company he founded, Alpha Natural Resources, Mike gave it to his hundreds of employees. When I asked him why, his answer was simple. "They are the reason I am successful."

That he and I can now be friends collaborating on coalfield goals was certainly a long shot back in the day when I represented landowners against every coal company he ever worked for as CEO. I also represented a local UMWA official, Sam Church (a man among men and at one time the president of the international UMWA), who was accused of assaulting Mike on his own company property during the strike.

I have to say as an aside that Sam did not make my job easier when he came to court sporting a homemade camouflaged tee shirt his buddies put together that depicted him literally carrying out the attack in a cartoonish manner. Sam would not change shirts as I requested, but finally consented to wear a work coat over it before the judge and Mike could see it.

Sam has since passed on, but for as long there is a UMWA, he will be honored. The following photo is courtesy of Tim C. Cox (tim@timccox.com).

SAM CHURCH

As I advance in age and become more nostalgic about and appreciative of purpose-driven lives, I have come to value and respect many, many coal company owners and UMWA leaders alike. Sam felt the same way, and together this mix of unlikely allies has gotten good things done for the Virginia coalfields. Additionally, a cadre of public agencies, individuals, and public officials has added several opportunities we never envisioned. Coalfield Virginia is truly a very big village. Ask any objective legislator in the state, and they will say that our region has the most cohesive, cooperative, and job-recruiting legislative team in the Commonwealth. That doesn't mean everyone agrees on all things, but when it comes to helping our region in general, they congeal like molasses on ice.

Although generational wealth is rare in the Virginia coalfields, the locals who make it big often exercise their Appalachian-based sense of generosity and community service. Coalfield Appalachia needs many more locally owned businesses to support a sustained comeback. It will happen when investors looking for a very welcoming atmosphere give us a chance. Despite these individual efforts, the huge loss of good-paying, middle-class, coal extraction and processing jobs holds back generations of smart young people from achieving the goal of economic security.

But allow me to be blunt: neither we nor our successors can make a game-changing dent without lots of help. There are successful women and men throughout Appalachia who work together as best as they can for young people and future generations. But to really make systemic change, state and federal policy makers, corporate America, and the media will need to be fair and open-minded about embedded cultural smears and negative preconceptions. Doing so will allow our kids, grandkids, and great-grandkids to show their stuff.

So, given this long history of racial and ethnic inclusion, the Appalachian soldiers who helped win our nation's wars, and the miners who dug coal and lost countless lives in violent accidents, there is a simple question I pose. Don't we at least deserve the respect of the keyboard warriors and urban political pundits who now revile and defame us? I think so, or I would not have authored this book.

When debates arise about fossil fuels and the jobs that are lost due to the decline of their uses, some critics of coal and natural gas production fail to understand that they can hate the carbon but should at least empathize with the loss of life-sustaining jobs. These middle-class-paying jobs engender self-respect. They also protect against the lonesome and very scary feeling of leaving a generational sense of home behind to start all over again in a foreign environment.

To hate someone's legal pursuit of financial opportunity should not equate to hate of the person. The ramifications are apparent as such elitist attitudes create resentment; furthermore, that resentment felt by millions of rural voters has political consequences, which in turn cause even further polarization.

In other words, Americans should not literally hate each other over differences of political opinions or the pursuit of legal occupations. It is a recipe for disaster.

Let's be honest. The worldwide green movement is gaining much momentum due to ever-evolving technology, not name-calling. It took a while for our ancestors to accept the horseless carriage, by the way. I was threatened and shot at for supporting federal controls on coal strip-mining in 1975-77, back when state legislators and statewide office seekers cared nothing about impacted coalfield residents (except for campaign contributions they received from coal companies). But each law that I supported resulted in more jobs, not fewer. Environmentalists need that pro-jobs kind of attitude today if they truly wish to cool down the rhetoric. Hopefully, green organizations will come to care about jobs other than their own. The Nature Conservancy is a good model for this type of collaboration.

To make our situation worse, cynics in both national political parties lament that public funds spent on the so-called "war on poverty" are not moving the needle far and fast enough. They cite statistics that indicate that after fifty years and billions of dollars spent, the nation's poverty rate has only moved downward three percent. Those numbers imply that a half-century of effort simply proves that poor people do not want to help themselves and their families.

Statistics are valuable tools only if all factors are considered, and this particular statistic leaves out one devastating piece of truth. During this same time period, our country signed off on lop-sided trade agreements with foreign countries that do not come close to adopting and enforcing our nation's work-safety and environmental laws. As a result, the USA has lost MILLIONS of good-paying middle-income jobs, and that loss has forced most of those Americans into poverty. In other words, but for the war on poverty, the declining status of poor people would be off the chart. Bottom line, the war on poverty is being fought in a vacuum and to just write it off as a failure does not take into account the rapid drop in jobs such as mining, steel and auto production, and numerous other skilled trades. Bring those jobs back, and poverty stats will shrink on their own. Are there really many Americans who believe that "made in China" comes anywhere near our history of quality products? And do we feel comfortable that millions of women, children, and minorities are being pushed to the brink with little pay in countries that do not care one whit about workers or the planet's environment?

So yes, coalfield residents take great umbrage when talking heads, with good jobs and oozing with privilege, declare that the abolition of coal mining is the only answer. Before coal mining is no more, shouldn't the nation's investors and policy makers help create good job opportunities before the majority of able-bodied adults and their children leave the coalfield region for good? That would be much more politically correct than continuing to disenfranchise rural American voters who feel like second-class cousins compared to suburban and urban dwellers.

Another news alert: rural people get out and vote, particularly in far Southwest Virginia. Just look at Virginia's 2021 gubernatorial race results as a reminder. As Virginia was becoming ever bluer, the unfamiliar changes pushed by the new majority were force-fed very quickly, and voters hit the brakes by electing conservative leaders to the top three statewide positions. Pragmatic voters never want one party to be the hard left or hard right automatic winners; too many constitutional rights are burned at the stake. Rodney King got it right when he asked, "Why can't we all just get along?" And that came from a Black man after he was beaten like a rabid dog.

Our country has repeatedly experienced what can happen when whole populations feel disenfranchised. Witness Joe Biden, a president from the anthracite coalfields of Pennsylvania, advocating for innovative job creations in the coalfields, one of the hardest-hit regions of America.

If successful, these overdue efforts will be compared to his predecessor who promptly tried to defund the Appalachian Regional Commission, a lifeline to the coalfields. This dedicated, single-purpose federal agency, founded in 1965, has built thousands of miles of primary country roads; installed countless water and sewer lines and facilities; updated housing and provided the world's fastest internet services in key mountain communities; supported and funded better hospitals, clinics, and dental care; and promoted educational programs geared toward job creation and leadership. The list goes on, and the uncaring effort to kill this program should not be forgotten.

Hopefully, the result of these recent economic incentives and additional support for federal and state agencies to draw good jobs to a region that has been directly hit by a local depression will be successful. Then many goal-oriented expatriates from these mountains will come back "home." The mountains are already experiencing an influx of talented folks from afar looking for a less stressful life, and that trend needs to be facilitated. We are seeing some of that influx due to violent crime and extreme weather disasters throughout the rest of the nation.

I may not live to see it, but I look forward to an epiphany among citizens in the disenfranchised rural areas of America that will cause them to team up politically with disenfranchised residents of inner cities and other struggling venues. The hope is that together they will vigorously pursue the quest for good jobs and improved education, and the prosperity, security, and pride they bring.

The ONLY way to change generational poverty is to establish generational wealth, which must include attracting, becoming, and supporting community-minded entrepreneurs. Neither major political party would like to see such a movement; they would begrudgingly have to switch their divisive tactics from blatant demagoguery to careful listening.

In other words, high-level political leaders are all so happy to stir up trouble among poor Americans by promising the moon and demonizing their fellow impoverished Americans. The reward received by the politicos playing this cynical game means that struggling citizens will cancel out each other's votes. It is a racket.

In summary, the coalfields of Appalachia are known and respected by mountain elders and some historians for many of their residents' opposition to slavery and inhumane working conditions. Thousands perished to preserve the Union during the Civil War, and later on, too many deaths led them to create another kind of union to make their ultra-dangerous trade much safer for their children and grandchildren.

It is not a far stretch to claim that our Appalachian coal region was literally the original home of the progressive movement when that policy meant supporting working men and women and respecting the differences among us. Coalfield Appalachians, for example, supported FDR, John Kennedy, Jay Rockefeller, and many other forward-thinking candidates. West Virginia, for example, literally salvaged Kennedy's campaign during a two-to-one primary vote that went his way.

John F. Kennedy campaigning in West Virginia

The History and Culture of Coalfields Southwest Virginia

OUR STRUGGLE TO gain a decent living in the mountains is an all-hands-on-deck village effort, now that the beast of living-wage joblessness reigns. No longer should we be viewed (or view ourselves) as throw-away people, and our landscape considered to be a national sacrifice zone.

So a memo from the Hillbilly Firewall is in order to our fellow Americans living outside of coalfield Appalachia, and to the talking heads who negatively assume too much (or too little) about our mountain character. To-wit: look at the race, gender, and labor relations histories of the place you call home and research the comparative academic achievements in your neck of the woods. Then stand them all up alongside ours, and with all due respect, find another whipping boy.

Until then, kindly send job opportunities to coalfield Appalachia. Our youth will show what they can do with mid-to-high skilled tech tasks and advanced manufacturing. This life-changing gesture we request will not be a handout; it is simply a challenge to re-evaluate preconceived negative attitudes and help those who are willing to help themselves. "Work" in our mountain culture is not yet a dirty four-letter word.

PART II
THE NATURAL AND SOCIAL HISTORY OF FAR SOUTHWEST VIRGINIA

CHAPTER 10
TRULY, THE VERY BEGINNING OF THE APPALACHIAN COALFIELDS

> AUTHOR'S NOTE: Chapters 1-9 touched upon current and recent events in our coalfield region. The following chapters are a chronological order of our more ancient past.

MANY PEOPLE HAVE LEARNED that Appalachia is one of the most ancient mountain chains in the world, and at its peak of upward thrusting our region's present-day mountains likely exceeded Mount Everest and its neighbors in height and grandeur. Millions and millions of years later, Appalachia's sharp peaks and surrounding high elevation plateaus succumbed to earth's natural forces. Water, and lots of it, in the form of snow, rain, wind, and sleet, combined with the ever-present cycles of seasonal heat and cold, did their jobs. These agents of physics fissured rock inch by inch, year to year, century to century, millennium to millennium, and mega-annum to mega-annum. Slowly but surely this process, assisted by gravity, inexorably whittled off the highest points and chipped the sky-high topography away to its present-day rounded shapes and vegetative covers.

This plate-tectonics process continues every minute of every day and will take the earth into a future we cannot even grasp. Our mountainous region will be far removed from its present longitude and latitude and become a water-sodden plain waiting to be uplifted again or folded into the ocean floors. But until then, let's take a look at our Appalachian region as paleo-geologists envision it was 350 million years ago in a conglomerate of the earth's plates we now call Pangea.

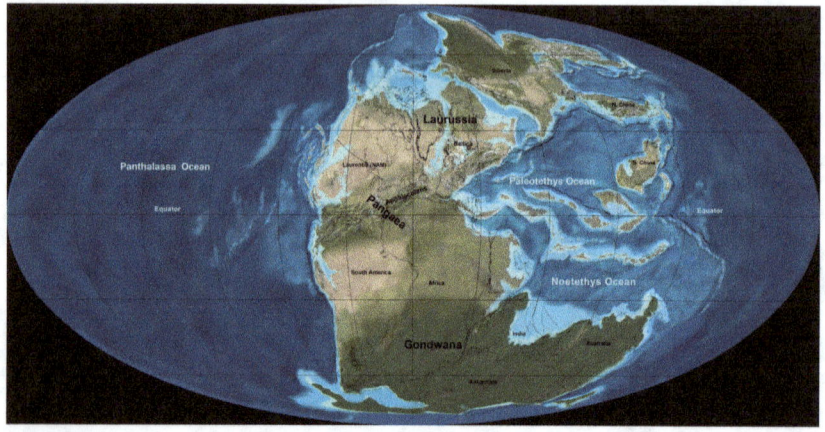

Pangea

If you are one of those people that often ask "why" and "how," you will enjoy this query: How did so much massive vegetation grow and then become coal given that Appalachia today is in a temperate climate zone where seasonal winter and cold would have retarded such astounding plant growth? The answer is in the map above.

During their formation, the present-day Appalachian Mountains and the massive swamps that preceded them were situated at or near the equator and started out as vast bog-like super troughs in a tropical climate perfect for supporting the lushest forests the planet has likely ever experienced. Today's Amazon Basin would probably pale in comparison. The above rendition of Pangea 350,000,000 years ago is a customized version of one that first appeared in textbooks. I contacted the paleo-geologist that drew the original map to superimpose the names of today's continents, the rising Appalachian Mountains, and the equator. This "temporary" location map placing today's Appalachian coalfields in tropical climates during the coal-forming process explains the conditions necessary to grow the multi-trillions of trees and understory that flourished in the massive swamps, bogs, and peat moss beds *predating* this map.

The History and Culture of Coalfields Southwest Virginia

These decaying swamps flourished in the Appalachian Basin, which experienced multiple growth layers as rising and receding inland seas deposited intermittent sand and mud strata. The mud strata supported intervening forests that slowly decayed and sank under their own weight, resulting in mega-massive peat-moss bogs. Sand layers several feet thick emerged as inland seas continued to rise and fall. Eventually, these sand strata dried out due to receding water, downward weight, and the resulting unimaginable pressure. Then the hardening sand compressed the layers of peat moss below that first formed into lignite and then bituminous coal.

The eastern edges of these vast coal seams were under lateral pressures thanks to plate tectonics (where present day North America and North Western Africa clashed) that caused an upward push of flat terrain into mountains, a process called orogeny. The preexisting bituminous coal then could harden into anthracite coal depending upon its location. Simply put, this means that under the pressures of heat and/or friction the impurities of those eastern coal beds were substantially squeezed out to produce a more pure, harder, "smokeless" coal. Such a transition turns sedimentary coal into metamorphic rock. The flammable carbon is still there, but the anthracite is usually a naturally purer coal. Therefore the western coal seams did not morph into anthracite due to the lack of intense pressure during their formation.

To better understand the geology and mining of Virginia's western non-anthracite coal, the following illustrations of a bituminous coal seam and deep mine in Appalachia may help.

> This cutaway drawing below is of a coal seam being mined block-by-block and pillar-by-pillar as part of a multipage colorized pamphlet produced by the Clinchfield Coal Company over a century ago. The landscape-style large handout was designed to recruit workers and investors, tout the built-from-scratch modern community of Dante in western Russell County, Virginia, and educate buyers and users of coal as to the dependability of this major source of fuel during the nation's Industrial Revolution, World War I, and eventually World War II.

Imaginary view of the inside of a mountain, illustrating the arrangement of entries, cross-entries, pillars, and rooms of a coal mine

Coal buggies being pulled from a coal mine to the outside by an electrical motor, a big advance over the older, more primitive methods such as miners pushing coal cars (aka buggies) by hand or pulling them by mules, donkeys, goats and even dogs. Bottom Right: Flashlight view of the junction of two entries Bottom left: coal being brought to the outside

The History and Culture of Coalfields Southwest Virginia

An electric machine undercutting a channel along the base of the seam

Bottom Left: Hand drilling for a black powder shot after undercutting Bottom Right: Loading mine cars at face of seam. Note the young boys operating a coal cutting machine. Child labor was widespread in the United States, particularly during the labor-starved Industrial Revolution.

A "trip" of loaded coal cars en route to an incline. The coal would then be "end dumped," and by gravity would slide down the chute for loading onto coal car railroad hoppers, sometimes forming a train a mile long pulled by steam locomotives (or diesel-powered engines decades later) to the next destination.

Eventually, Pangea broke apart due to ever-evolving sea floor plate shifting and spreading, aided by resulting surface and underwater earthquake activities and volcanic eruptions. As a result, what we today call coalfield Appalachia came to a temporary rest in its present location.

The word *temporary* in geologic terms is relative; the earth's surface never comes to a complete standstill, nor was Pangea formed, then separated, by sudden violent shifts of the earth's crust alone. Thus, the process known as *plate tectonics* is mostly minuscule pushes, shoves, and sinking and rising motions that culminate in fractions of time and distance. When the earth's crust can stand the frictional heat and pressure no more, volcanoes form below the earth's surface; sometimes breaching the surface with fire, brimstone, and volcanic cones, and at other times thrusting huge blocks of solid rock seams skyward without spewing lava onto the surface. Then the more sudden and spectacular break-ups and movements of today's remnants of Pangea occur.

Add to all this commotion continental and regional glaciations that have intermittently bulldozed huge swaths of the landscape for millions of years, and you can only imagine the flora, fauna, and cultures that came before us. Six billion years of earth's multiple iterations could have spawned beings potentially much superior to *Homo sapiens* that ended up dying from natural disasters or gained the technology to wipe out each other in a day. It is very arrogant to assume that we humans are Nature's best creation of all time. Surely not.

So the current location of Appalachia will change, and is changing, although the many geologic fault-lines we see evidence of today as we dig through ancient rock and carbon are technically "dead." The collateral geologic pressures at play today will eventually transport our little part of the world westward as North America rides along an Asia-bound conveyor belt of geologic forces that we yet do not fully comprehend. In other words, Pangea, in other earthly locations and configurations, will reappear and the whole process will then repeat itself.

Below is a view of the St. Paul Fault, an overturning thrust fault just south of the Dominion power plant in St. Paul, Virginia, on Route 58-A. It is rare to see such a unique fault line from a busy public road. The fault was the result of billion-plus-years-old deep limestone strata being overthrust atop the eastern edge of much younger (200,000,000 or so years) sand, siltstone, and coal strata. This fault line runs northeast to southwest through three states. In Virginia it roughly divides the limestone ridge and valley farmlands to the east from the much more narrow coal-bearing hollows, hills, and dendritically eroded plateaus to the west. The 70-million-year-old Clinch River runs along this fault line in far Southwest Virginia

This ancient river, one of the cleanest in the East, is unique because it hosts the most abundant concentration of rare and endangered freshwater aquatic life in the nation. These aquatic species and subspecies are studied by scientists from around the world. An ecology center in St. Paul, Virginia, managed by the University of Virginia, guides and houses scientists, graduate students, and state and federal agency personnel as the waters become warmer and the need to protect and sometimes reproduce these species emerges. A few of these species, including mussels, are found only in the Clinch River Valley watershed, while other durable survivors live in neighboring rivers (Powell and Holston) that together make up Virginia's largest source of headwaters flowing into the Tennessee Valley Watershed.

St. Paul Fault: Over-turning thrust fault along Route 58-A near Dominion's power plant, St. Paul, Virginia

Closer view of thrust fault near St. Paul, Virginia

The History and Culture of Coalfields Southwest Virginia

Clinch River rare and endangered freshwater mussels (photo courtesy of Virginia's coolest agency, the Department of Conservation and Recreation)

CHAPTER 11
THE ICE AGE IN COALFIELD APPALACHIA

The most recent great change in our region's flora and fauna came about during the latest Ice Age, which began about 15,000 years ago. This intense cold spell lasted off and on for approximately 5,000 years before the current big thaw began. At its most southern edge, continental glaciers formed in the Arctic region all the way down to present day mid-Pennsylvania.

The warming and cooling of the earth's surface is a well-documented, oft-repeated natural phenomenon. By studying geological strata, petrified forests, and thousand-year-old living trees, scientists from various disciplines can trace our planet's ever-changing climate and its history.

No doubt human activities for the past few thousands of years, more particularly the most recent 150 years, have impacted the earth's atmosphere, but to what degree we cannot definitively calculate. For example, present day Antarctica is a frozen wasteland to most observers; yet recent deep-soil sampling proves that 90,000,000 years ago it was covered by a tropical forest. During that period, this now-frigid continent was not close enough to the equator to support such lush vegetation. So the very early explanation is that the earth was overall much warmer then than now and had much more carbon dioxide in the atmosphere. Why and how? These are mysteries difficult to unravel and, although very informative, such findings likely will not help our present-day global warming situation.

Instead of calling each other names as scientists from polar opposite camps drone on, let's just stipulate that clean air is good for all animal life, including humans, and that benefit alone is worth working toward more life-giving oxygen and less carbon dioxide and methane. In doing so, the people who risked and lost their lives in the coal mining industry to propel this country forward as the world's leading industrial powerhouse should not be dishonored and left behind. There were no feasible alternatives during the fast-paced Industrial Revolution to fuel such massive world development. Now our coal miners and their descendants are at a loss as to why they are being attacked and marginalized by a big-city white-collar culture that prides itself as being wholly inclusive. Surely this irony is obvious.

The most recent Ice Age and the many iterations that came before it did not come about due to human activities, but it certainly had an impact upon human migratory routes around the world. Slowly but surely our predecessors migrated toward warmer climates and more plentiful game and forage.

The Ice Age caused the earth's oceans to recede and lower in great depths as trillions of tons of water compacted and shrank into ice. Lots of ice. Pre-Ice Age mammals that could not make the cold weather cut —or head south and adapt quickly enough—evolved into larger species, subspecies, and varieties that were more efficient in storing body heat. The species that did not adapt or evolve simply died out. Their evolving successors much later became known to us as megafauna that roamed the Northern Hemisphere looking for scarce forage in large herbivore herds. Likewise, the oversized carnivorous predators prowled in vicious packs relentlessly hunting for food, including humans. Our ancestors had to be stealthy and pick off the weaker vegetarian strays, while the large wolves and cats were mostly off the menu. Wooly mammoth, mastodons, caribou, bison, saber-toothed cats, cave bears, dire wolves, wild horses, huge red deer, great elk, very large ground sloths, oversized porcupines, cow-sized beavers, and musk oxen abounded. Cold weather birds emerged, including the beautiful snowy owl.

The forests that could grow in this frozen tundra, in what we now call Appalachia, covered the valleys and ridges with cold-resistant evergreens such as fir, spruce, cedar, and hemlock. Some of the last remnants of these boreal forests exist today on Beartown Mountain in Russell County, and its exact namesake in Tazewell County, both part of the Clinch Mountain range. This solidified sandstone-capped folded mountain rises like a rock fortress wall just east of the Virginia coalfields. Farther east, the taller mountains of Whitetop and Mt. Rogers host thousands of these trees, as do the Great Smoky Mountains in Tennessee and North Carolina. The Smokies are the high point of the entire Appalachian range, and back in the day likely rivaled the height of Mount Everest and its neighbors. Millions and millions of years of erosion lowered the Appalachian Mountains down to the mere roots we see today while Mt. Everest is still growing higher as the Earth's moving plates push those ridges upward.

High mountain bogs and wetlands formed in the more shallow depressions found in the taller Appalachian Mountains, and many of them are still intact. The most prominent one in a Virginia coalfield county is Tazewell's Beartown Mountain:

Beartown Wilderness

Beartown Wilderness was established in 1984 in eastern Tazewell County. This 5,609-acre treasure is not only one of the most remote locations in Virginia, it is also, without a doubt, unique in all of Virginia because it is home to fast flowing streams, significant stands of rare old-growth communities, outstanding views, and a sphagnum bog.

Roaring Fork, a rushing stream running through the middle of Beartown, is a designated cold water stream and home to native brook trout. A journey along Roaring Fork is exceedingly difficult. Rhododendron hells line the stream from its modest beginning all the way to the southeastern boundary. Only a fool would choose to walk its length. Cove Branch begins in a bog located between Clinch Mountain, the backbone of Beartown Wilderness and of Garden Mountain to the east. The branch meanders lazily through meadows of ferns, grasses, cranberries, and hazel trees before plunging 1,400 feet to Roaring Fork. Barkcamp Branch and Coon Branch are the other two major tributaries of Roaring Branch. Both have their beginning high on Clinch Mountain and drop rapidly to Roaring Branch.

Roaring Branch begins on the southern rim of Burkes Garden. The Garden is a high sheltered cove completely surrounded by Garden Mountain. Beartown Mountain, at 4,680 feet, is the highest point on Garden Mountain and in the Beartown Wilderness. On the summit is a wonderful meadow surrounded by a stand of slow-growing red spruce. There are also several other peaks that soar above the 4,000-foot level. Clinch Mountain climbs to 4,600 feet. Hutchinson Rock near the extreme northwest point of Garden Mountain stands at 4,450 feet. Not too far from Hutchinson Rock is the hole-in-the-rock-wall. The summit of Chestnut Ridge (4,400 feet) is just outside the wilderness boundary. At the crest of this ridge is a stone Appalachian Trail shelter located in the meadow. The view from the hut is nothing short of amazing.

The flora of Beartown Wilderness is spectacular. Near the southern boundary there is oak-hickory forest, so common in the mountains of Virginia. However, at higher elevations, the forest changes to northern hardwoods and spruce. On the ridge leading to the summit of Garden Mountain are significant stands of old growth, including yellow birch in all sorts of twisted, gnarled forms. Many of these trees possess unique root structures with tendrils that seemingly support the trunk in the air. This phenomenon is the result of birch seeds germinating on a decaying log that then rots away to leave the aerial birch. The red spruce is also making a comeback on Garden Mountain. Thickets of young red spruce are a common sight on the ridge crest. Fraser Magnolia is found in scattered pockets along Roaring Fork.

Then there is the bog. Protected by near-impenetrable stands of rhododendron and thickets of cranberry and hazel, a journey into the bog is nearly impossible. The bog lies near the summit of two high ridges. This protective cove harbors a multitude of rare species.

There is only one trail in Beartown Wilderness. However, the Appalachian Trail follows along the southern boundary of the wilderness through the meadows located on the crest of Chestnut Ridge.

1) Roaring Branch Trail, 1.7 miles (one-way)
2) AT, 2.5 miles (one-way)

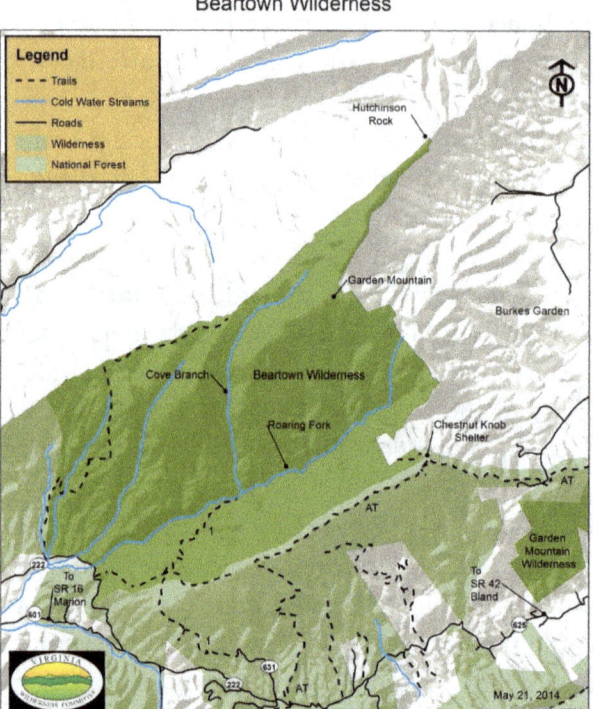

Courtesy of Virginia Dept of Wildlife Resources, DWR

The following photos of the Beartown Mountain bogs were taken by the author in 2010.

One of the many bog ponds

One of the many bog ponds

Early fall hues tinge ferns and native grass

Beaver-dammed pond

U.S. Coast and geodetic survey marker

RUSSELL COUNTY HOSTED a similar swampy wetlands before the high elevation valley area was dammed up to create the Laurel Bed Lake. Below are aerial photos of the 330-acre lake. After a non-scientific poll, it seems that most Russell Countians do not realize this stunning body of water is in their county and relatively few have visited it.

> NOTE: The author worked with multiple stakeholders to build a road to Laurel Bed Lake from Russell County that will greatly reduce the one-hour arduous drive through Smyth County and then a narrow gravel road that is prone to slide down the ravines and be closed in the winter months.

Aerial photo by Tommy Shrader

The History and Culture of Coalfields Southwest Virginia

Aerial photo by Tommy Shrader

The first evidence of human activity in far Southwest Virginia was found in and near the town of Saltville, and the hunters and gatherers of those days were predecessors of the Folsom Paleo-Indian cultures of 13,000-14,000 years ago. Some paleontologists assert that humans first came from Siberia to what we now know as America during this period of frozen seas by crossing the Bering Strait "bridge." This feature was actually a barren rock ridge linking the two continents that only exposes itself when the oceans recede due to the massive icing that periodically occurs.

Others believe there is proof of an earlier wave of migration from what is now western Asia and Russia as long as 30,000 years ago, but evidence for that is scant. Even more recently improved DNA testing implies that some Native American ancestors arrived from the Pacific Islands by boat. This theory, if proved, would be a game changer for the land bridge theorists.

The task of reaching back that far in time is difficult. Could it be a combination of Siberian residents of Asian descent who came by land and watercraft and Pacific Islanders known for far-reaching open sea voyages? Emerging DNA technology suggests just that. Glaciation has a way of scrubbing evidence away from modern *Homo sapiens'* inquisitive eyes. But clues still exist.

In any event, today's Native Americans (more correctly called American Indians or Indigenous Americans when not referring to a specific community, visit https://americanindian.si.edu/nk360/faq/did-you-know for more) are the progeny of many early immigrants seeking a better life. Sound familiar?

These Old World immigrants who came by foot across the Arctic region, or by boat from warmer environs, could not have known or even fathom that thousands of years later their descendants would first clash with immigrants from across the Atlantic Ocean, likely starting with the Vikings, and end up clashing with people from around the globe as they were drawn to the so-called New World.

The only proof of Ice Age animals found nearest the Virginia coalfields is from a 1993 dig on a Russell County farm (once owned by the author) on the western flanks of the Clinch Mountains. The new owner decided to dig a fish pond in a small bog. While doing so, his workers noticed fragments of what were later scientifically identified as mammoth and mastodon tusks, teeth, knee bones, and other fragments.

It is unusual to find both mammoth and mastodon bones at the same site; the difference of the two is that mastodons were smaller with straighter tusks and ate woody plants which required sharper molars, while the larger mammoths foraged on grass and had flatter molars to grind the softer food. See below (Courtesy U.S. National Park Service).

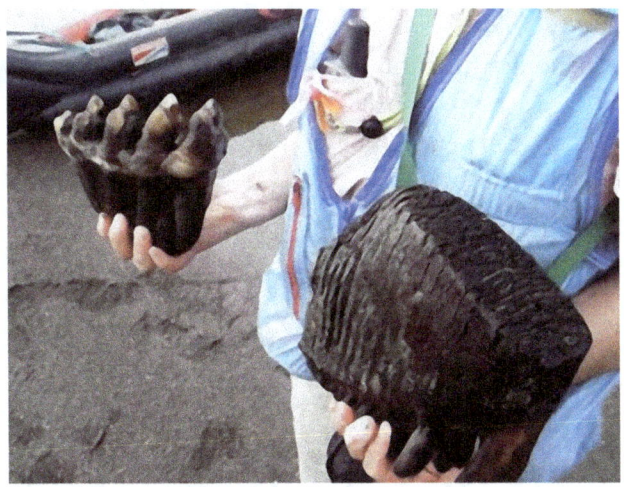

Mastodon vs mammoth molars

Mastodon, left, and wooly mammoths, right

Some of the deeper finds at the Russell County excavation site were wood fragments near the bones that were carbon dated at 29,000 to 32,000 years ago. There likely were no humans in our neck of the woods around the time these massive animals got caught in an alluvial landslide or simply ventured too far into a muddy, clay-filled bog and got stuck. Some scientists will say absolutely that man was not present anywhere in the Western Hemisphere at that time, but really, how would we know that for sure? Declarations of the "oldest" findings of plants and animals are repeatedly bested by even more evidence from new digs, excavations, and technology.

Evidence of human versus mastodons and mammoths is found worldwide as well as in the Saltville, Virginia, dig. Charred animal bones were discovered in what resembled a firepit there, making a reasonable hypothesis that humans may have cooked a meal way back in the day. Local retired boxer, musician, and artist, Darris Stanley, envisions one such encounter in what is now known as the Appalachian coalfields.

Artwork by Darris Stanley

Very few mastodon and mammoth bones have ever been found in Virginia. The digs in Russell County and Saltville have yielded the state's most intact remains thus far, and it is likely that these finds are only the tip of the iceberg, so to speak. Unfortunately, some of the Russell County relics were borrowed from the landowners to never be returned, or the returned samples deteriorated because the borrowers did not know how to preserve them. None of the tusk remains were returned intact. The Ratliff family preserved the remaining bones and fragments with great care and had them (until recently) displayed at their home which was built next to the dig site. A scientific summary and the resulting photos below are the only formal record of this extraordinary event.

> Mastodon remains recovered by Dr. Charles Bartlett and associates from the Ratcliff Site, Russell County, Virginia, are pictured below. Also see the following article by Whittecar, Wynn, and Bartlett, 2007, Quaternary Research 68:133-140, (printed with permission).

The History and Culture of Coalfields Southwest Virginia

Well-preserved mastodon tooth

A landowner in 1993 decided to dig a pond on his farm in Russell County, Virginia, near the coalfields of southwestern Virginia, and came upon a very rare find. The dig site lies south of the north slope of Clinch Mountain, the crest of which marks the division line between Washington (southward) and Russell counties. The recovery site was in a deep natural trench underlain by a massive debris flow that originated in the valley that filled the mouth of the trench. A series of extremely large torrential rain storms that passed across this mountain in the past 40,000+ years built this debris fan which clogged the small valley and created ponds and wetlands that preserved the mastodon and mammoth bones.

Four of the mastodon teeth recovered from the Ratcliff site

In-situ large fragment of a pelvis from a mammoth excavated at about nine meters (twenty-nine feet) deep in the excavated trench.

The end fragment of a mastodon or mammoth tusk partially coated with bright blue vivianite, an aluminum phosphate mineral coating deposited later.

Dr. Charles Bartlett of Abingdon, Virginia, shown at a public press conference held at the dig site and holding a tusk fragment

View of the twenty-nine-foot-deep trench dug with a very large backhoe in preparation for constructing a dam for a trout pond on this land where the extinct animal bones were recovered. Four radiocarbon dates were obtained from wood extracted in the lower five feet of the trench, ranging from 29,100 +/- 300 B.P. years to 32,400 +/- 480 B.P. years.

[End of article]

UPDATE: The Ratliff family has donated these Ice Age relics to Mountain Heritage, a non-profit the author formed years ago. The bones rest in the Mountain Heritage Museum housed in the Kilgore Building in St. Paul, Virginia. The photos below show the new current resting place for these priceless remains of animals gone by. Preparations are being made to recruit a more sustainable coalfield institution to carry out the purposes of the museum.

New home for Ice Age relics

Close up of knee bone

The History and Culture of Coalfields Southwest Virginia

Close-up of molars and other bone fragments. the Native American artifacts in this photo were found on the same farm but are thousands of years younger than the bones.

CHAPTER 12
THE PETRA PROJECT

The following article is a fascinating more recent Ice Age find in Lee County, Virginia, regarding another Ice Age creature, this time a predator (reprinted with permission).

By Dave Socky
Posted October 14, 2021

Cave and karst scientists in the Virginia Department of Conservation and Recreation (DCR). This agency's Natural Heritage Division played a crucial role in the recent discovery and excavation of a fully preserved large cat skeleton in southwest Virginia. DCR karst protection coordinator Wil Orndorff and karst protection specialists Katarina Kosič Ficco and Tom Malabad were among the 11 cavers.

The History and Culture of Coalfields Southwest Virginia

Dr. Alex Hastings inspecting the skeleton in the cave.

Hiking through trees to the cave.

Tom Malabad carrying several cave packs into the cave.

Burja Cave, located in Lee County, Virginia, has been explored and mapped for a number of years and is still being pushed today. It is a vertical cave and quite sporting — the good leads are three to four hours into the cave. Before COVID hit, a large animal skeleton was discovered on one of the survey trips. Photos were taken and experts consulted. It was suspected it was some kind of cat and that it could be pretty old — thousands of years old. The skeleton was not small, about four feet long from head to pelvic bone.

After consultation with Dr. Alex Hastings, the Fitzpatrick Chair of Paleontology at the Science Museum of Minnesota (and the former Virginia Museum of Natural History Assistant Curator of Paleontology and a caver, of course), it was decided that the skeleton was worth collecting so further study could take place. In order to make the skeleton more personable and easier to discuss, Alex suggested it be given a name. Thus, it was decided to call it "Petra," a word derived from the Greek word for rock or stone — *petros*.

Getting to the skeleton

On Thursday, a small group of cavers staged required material at the entrance to the cave. The cave is accessed by bushwhacking through the woods down a very steep mountainside for about a mile. In a couple of places there are unstable rocks covered with leaves on the steep slope, making for real tricky footing. The last one hundred feet down the hill was rigged with rope to be used as a hand line because of the steepness. I arrived Thursday evening at Natural Tunnel State Park. The project had rented the largest cabin at the park since we had a total of eleven participants for the weekend. My job was to videotape the process of skeleton removal so that an educational and conservation program could be produced.

Friday morning found the group climbing down the steep mountainside with packs and backpacks of gear, plus personal cave packs and vertical kits. Twenty feet into the entrance is the first pit, a forty-foot drop into a large breakdown filled chamber. From the chamber, we went through a short, wide crawl, which turned into a narrow, muddy low tunnel with a knee-wide slot in the floor. This went on for several hundred feet but eventually opened up to almost walking passage.

The next obstacle was a section of floorless canyon with a traverse line for safety. Then another forty-foot pit into a shallow pool of water. Across the room was a twelve-foot climbdown, rigged with a rope for safety. Then a nuisance drop of fifteen-feet and finally, after a short crawl, was the room where the skeleton was located. With all the gear and the large number of cavers, it took about an hour to get to the site.

The real work begins

Dr. Alex Hastings was now in charge, and, after stashing our packs and removing vertical gear, we got down to work. The first order of business was to take photos and measurements. Joe Myre took many high-resolution photos of the cat from various angles. Later, Joe will use the photos and a special computer program to construct 3D images of the skeleton.

Alex made a detailed sketch of the skeleton and wrote notes about its condition. He then performed a physical inspection to determine the condition of the skeleton. Until this time, we didn't know whether it was composed of solid, calcified bones or if it was soft and easily broken. If the bones were not solid, we had the material to make plaster casts. Using dental tools to poke and prod at the bones, Alex was able to determine that the bones were very solid. As a matter of fact, they were more or less welded in place in a thin layer of calcite surrounding the skeleton.

The whole skeleton was fully articulated and was all in one piece. It would have to be broken into pieces in order for it to be removed and packaged in packs that could be carried out of the cave.

Time to dig

Team meticulously digging around Petra.

Progress after digging for hours.

Once the condition of the skeleton was determined, the next task was to dig down into the rock and dirt around the bones. This task took up the better part of the whole day because it was accomplished using dental picks and small tools. As the perimeter was dug out, dirt and rock were removed from under the bones, so that eventually the skeleton was sticking out in relief with just a little material underneath for support. During this process, small pieces of material were dug out, at which point Alex would determine if they were bone or rock. If bone, we packaged them up in paper towels and then taped it in a sandwich of closed cell foam and bubble wrap. Each piece was marked with the project name, date, and location. After digging around and underneath, the tailbone, embedded in a thin layer of calcite, was eventually removed as one piece. It was about 2.5 feet long.

Later, the front leg bones were also detached and set aside. What was especially cool was seeing the inner section of the leg bone where it had broken off from the main skeleton. It was white, and inside the hollow section, you could see thin layers of crystallized material.

A look inside one of Petra's bones.

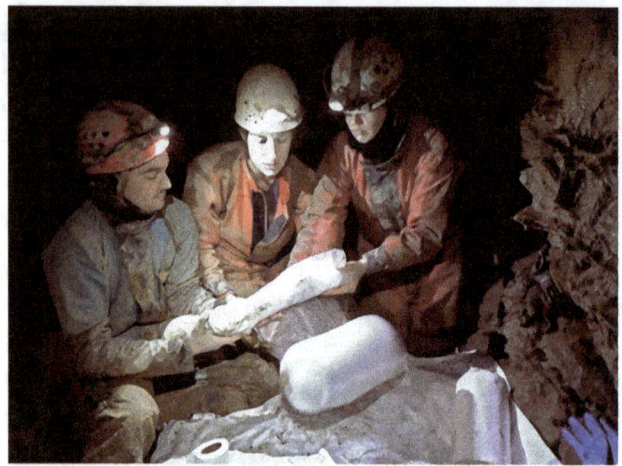

(L-R) Alex Hastings, Katarina Kosic Ficco, & Lauren Satterfield wrapping a leg bone.

A long day of work

At this point, it was getting late in the day, about 6:30 p.m. We took some measurements of the tail and leg bones to see what size boxes we would need on Saturday in order to package the different parts and pieces. We then put our vertical gear back on, packed up our gear, and headed out.

The location of the skeleton is not really that far from the entrance, but it is still challenging. The cave is very muddy, and the ropes get coated with mud. Our vertical gear was coated with mud. Cams didn't catch, so climbing out was a challenge. It took a couple of hours to get out, and then, of course, we had to climb back up the mountain in the dark. This was my first time up this hill, and I thought it would never end. We finally made it back to the cars around 10:30 p.m.

Packing up the cat

On Saturday morning, Mike Ficco and Tom Malabad drove all the way to a Walmart to get containers, towels, and bubble wrap, while the rest of us headed back into the cave. The weather was great, and we made it down the mountain, into the cave and to the skeleton site without any issues. While one group continued to dig around and under the bones, another group started in on the packaging task.

In order to protect the larger pieces, the bone was first laid on a shelf; then the upper exposed surface was covered with toilet paper. The toilet paper was sprayed with water and then molded to the surface of the bone. Another layer of toilet paper was added, sprayed and molded. More layers were added. It was kind of like a cast, where all the protruding parts were covered and protected, and the whole piece was encased in toilet paper!

The piece would then be rolled and taped in bubble wrap, and then finally encased in a thin layer of closed cell foam. Masking tape was used to hold everything together. The larger pieces were then wrapped in a thicker layer of closed cell foam (sleeping pad material from Walmart) and stuffed into large expedition cave packs. Some pieces, like the skull, were able to fit into large plastic containers, which were then stuffed with packing material to keep it locked in place.

One of the hardest things Alex had to contend with was deciding where and how to break parts of the skeleton. In some cases, the bones broke naturally, giving him no choice. In other cases, a hammer and chisel had to be used to force the issue. Sometimes the break would occur where desired, but in others the bone would break in unexpected locations. It had to be done, though, because there was no way the larger pieces could be moved out of the cave without damage.

The work was meticulous and time consuming, but, soon enough, all parts of the skeleton were separated and the only task remaining was to pack them with toilet paper and paper towels and surround them up with bubble wrap and package them up in packs and boxes. At one point, we thought we might run out of toilet paper and paper towels. Mike even offered to run out of the cave and make a store run for more, but that would have taken way too long. As it turned out, we had just the right amount. We used every roll of toilet paper and paper towels and finally finished the packaging around 9 p.m.

Everyone was very happy (especially Alex) that we had gotten the whole skeleton excavated and would be able to remove all the parts and pieces from the cave that day.

Exit strategy

Now, the significant task was to remove all the packs from the cave. Wil and Zenah Orndorff and Mike and Andrea Futrell had rigged the three drops with progress capture haul lines for pulling packs up the drops. It was decided we would haul everything up, making it easier and safer for everyone to climb out without having to tether packs. Mike and Andrea had already taken out several packs, but we still had twelve heavy mud-covered packs (some personal and some cat) to get out with only seven cavers to move them. We decided to do a caver chain, where we would string out in a line and then pass packs from person to person. Once all the packs were moved to the head of the line, we would move forward past the pile and repeat the process.

We finally got all the packs piled up at the bottom of the entrance drop. I thought it was about 10 p.m., but when I looked at my watch, I saw it was 12:30 a.m.! Wow, how time flies! It was 2 a.m. when we finally got up to the cars with all the bones. Not having enough cavers, we had to leave a number of packs at the entrance to the cave to be retrieved the next day. Sunday was pack retrieval day — in the rain. It wasn't too bad, and by early afternoon, we had retrieved all the packs, including my "lost" chest harness and croll, which had slid down a side drop at the entrance Friday evening.

Expedition successfully complete

It was a successful project expedition, with all the cat bones excavated and removed. Alex's first guess is that the cat is an "American cheetah," probably thousands of years old. However, he emphasized that this is a preliminary determination, and it's inconclusive until further studies are performed.

The Petra Project would not have been possible without the tremendous support of the Cave Conservancy of the Virginias, the Virginia Department of Conservation and Recreation Division of Natural Heritage, the Virginia Museum of Natural History, the Minnesota Science Museum, and the U.S. Forest Service.

The History and Culture of Coalfields Southwest Virginia

Dave Socky has been a project caver for 47 years. He serves as treasurer of the Blue Ridge Grotto, a member of the Board of Directors for the Cave Conservancy of the Virginias and president of the Virginia Speleological Survey.

A rendition of the North American Ice Age map approximately 18,000 years ago.

An American cheetah (Miracinonyx trumani) and her cubs crouch over the remains a Harrington's mountain goat (Oreamnos harringtoni) inside a cave in the Grand Canyon, while a Shasta ground sloth (Nothrotheriops shastensis) lumbers past and a California condor (Gymnogyps californianus) soars in the distance. Inside the cave, two Stock's vampire bats (Desmodus stocki) hang from the ceiling, and a woodrat (Neotoma) hides by the wall on the right. Ovoid structures on the cave floor are droppings left by ground sloths, based on finds in locations such as Rampart Cave. (Image credit: Illustration by Julius Csotonyi / Courtesy of National Park Service)

CHAPTER 13
NATIVE AMERICANS

Of Appalachia's Native Americans that first encountered Europeans in the Appalachian coalfields, most were members of several related and/or warring tribes.

The first Europeans most likely to have made contact with the Native Americans of Appalachia were the Spanish. Historians differ as to whether they penetrated present day Virginia at all, but unlike most mysteries this epic journey has been chronicled. The confusion comes about because the precise locations of physical points referred to in any ancient document are always a task to cipher.

Ruiz Hernando de Soto led a large Spanish army of 600 or so well-armed and armored conquistadors into southeastern North America in 1540. As for proof, an interpretive account of de Soto's discoveries is on record at the U.S. Library of Congress, filed as "The Final Report of the United States de Soto Expedition Commission, 76 Congress, 1 Sessions, and House Executive Document #7."

Hernando de Soto. Artwork by Darris Stanley

Conquistadors. Artwork by Darris Stanley

Let's assume the accuracy of historians who are convinced de Soto's entourage came into present day Southwest Virginia. Then, it had to be astounding as to what his soldiers, enslaved people, and a handful of priests found as they traveled along riverbanks northward from Florida to present-day Eastern Tennessee and Southwest Virginia. The expedition was looking mostly for gold, and the greediest soldiers among these participants terrorized the Native Americans they met with gunfire, sword, and more.

The invading men and animals (swine, war dogs, and horses) spread death and disease wherever they traveled. The commanders and soldiers took what they wanted and murdered Native Americans as if slaughtering vermin. Some historians concluded from the Spanish journals that de Soto's men came across Egyptian-type fortressed cities; there they found moats, chests filled with fresh-water pearls, and aristocratic societies within which women had substantial roles. The Spanish reports speak of a fortified capital of the Cafitachequi tribe on the banks of the Santee River in present day South Carolina, which the conquistadors referred to as the "Village of the Queen."

Closer to present-day Southwest Virginia, some researchers believe the expedition eventually found the headwaters of the Clinch River in what is now Tazewell County and that, at the time, a Native American tribe incorrectly dubbed the Xualan empire by the Spaniards turned out to be of the Cafitachequi Queendom.

These tribes, regardless of their proper names, built impressive walls of logs, rocks, and mud to heights of fifteen feet. Some of the towns were encircled by water-filled moats and featured large domed meeting halls in the center. Remnants of Native American villages similar to de Soto's descriptions were found in Tazewell County's Abbs Valley years ago, and smaller remnants were discovered on the Hendricks Farm in Russell County in the late 1800s. This sophisticated tribe had dwindled to a few survivors by 1671, when Captain Henry Batten came across a dozen or so ragtag members of the once-great nation selling salt at Wood's Gap in what is now Floyd County. Proving, once more, that European diseases by a long shot killed many more Native Americans than guns.

The humanity void created in Southwest Virginia as the Queendom disintegrated was quickly occupied by copious amounts of wildlife that flooded the Clinch River Valley. The neighboring coal-laden Cumberland Plateau also sat patiently to the west for millions of years, awaiting the European hordes who would cut and routinely export one of the most impressive virgin hardwood forests likely ever known. That seminal event occurred on such a grand scale from the mid-1800s to the mid-1900s that today, less than one percent of the old-growth forests remain in Appalachia. That human extractive undertaking was surpassed only by the mass removal of 200-million-year-old coal in untold amounts for more than a hundred years, starting in commercial earnest during the 1880s and tapering to a crawl by the 2020s.

An integrated lumbering crew in 1883, around the same time that vigorous coal mining began in the Appalachians

(A) Saw-mill and lumber-yards of the White Oak Lumber Co., at Honaker. A triple-band mill, with a capacity rated at 100,000 board feet per day. Its timber all comes from Dickenson and Buchanan counties.

The cutting and shipping of Appalachian logs and lumber worldwide reached an incredible scale.

The History and Culture of Coalfields Southwest Virginia

Shawnee, Cherokee, and Mingo also filled the void left by the Queendom's disappearance, but those tribes were not as sophisticated and dug-in as their somewhat mystical predecessors tended to be. However, they did establish or expand hunting routes, maintained multi-year hunting camps and substantial, but not permanent, villages along the banks of the Upper Clinch River and, to a lesser degree, the Big Sandy tributaries to the west. Large, "permanent" Cherokee towns were likely not established in what is now Southwest Virginia, as some in our region seem to believe, because to do so with the war-like Shawnee on the prowl was not feasible or sustainable. If Kentucky, once a mere county of Virginia, was the "dark and bloody ground," then far Southwest Virginia was the precursor of that slaughter to come between settlers from the United Kingdom and Germany versus literally outgunned natives. These newcomers were in direct competition with roaming hunting parties of braves and chieftains looking for game and highly profitable furs.

Although the French government was much more humane in dealing with the Natives than the much sterner English, there was a period when Cherokee leaders became celebrities in the United Kingdom. That major tribe of the Appalachian Mountains was won over by King George II in 1730. Called "the warlords of Southwest Virginia," the Cherokee were a fiercely independent people, as were the European immigrants that relentlessly pushed them westward. Sir Alexander Cuming, a cocky diplomat from King George's court, ultimately garnered the Natives' allegiance. After many powwows, a truce between the two parties emerged. The King proclaimed that no more White settlers could claim land west of the Blue Ridge Mountains; the Cherokee depended on his word.

Sir Cuming took seven Cherokee leaders and their interpreter to England on the HMS Man-Of-War *Fox* on May 4, 1730. They were treated like royalty and witnessed the great British Army on maneuvers, its heavy weapons in action, and the British fleet with its large cannons and billowing sails. The North American visitors were rightfully awestruck.

AUTHOR'S NOTE: For readers who wish to review the London newspaper articles regarding the arrival and long stay of these Cherokee leaders during two separate trips, those very interesting stories are accessible at CherokeeRegistry.com)

BELOW IS one such British newspaper article and illustrations about their visit.

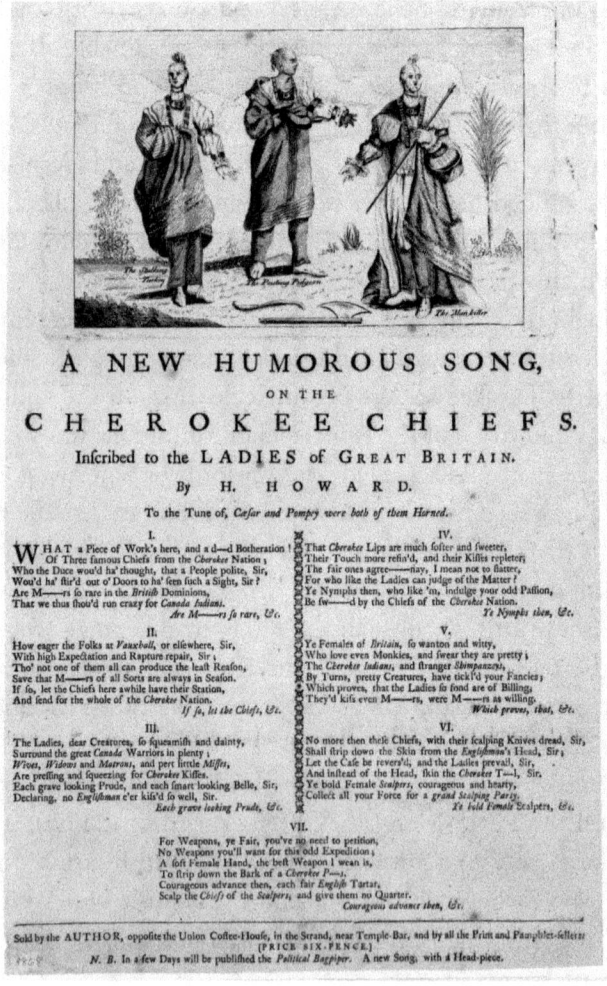

Article from a London newspaper about the Cherokee visitors

When the Cherokee "royalty" returned home to their towns in present-day North Carolina and Tennessee, they were confident that their remaining territory was safe because King George II of England had told them so. Peace between the English and Native Americans didn't last very long, however. The French, centuries-long rivals of England, began siding with local Native tribes to push back English incursions into the French-claimed Great Lakes territory where that country's fur trade established an almost endless supply of wealthy endeavors.

The first significant French/English skirmish in America happened in 1754, when Virginia militiamen (mostly mustered from its western region, including what is now West Virginia) under the command of twenty-two-year-old George Washington ambushed a French patrol while they were eating and resting. In other words, they were bushwhacked. This tactic caused an international stir among western Europeans because at that time the military leaders of both countries believed in rules of war that did not include sneak attacks or Native American-style guerrilla tactics. Many of those genteel rules of military engagement changed that day.

The population of America's British colonies leading up to the French and Indian War is helpful in understanding the mix of races, immigrants, and centers of commerce and political power at the time. The map below depicts the world's first known country that was purposely formed by the mixing of cultures and races from across the Western world and beyond. (For example, Native Filipino slaves known as Luzonians were brought to the West Coast as early as 1587 by the Spanish.)

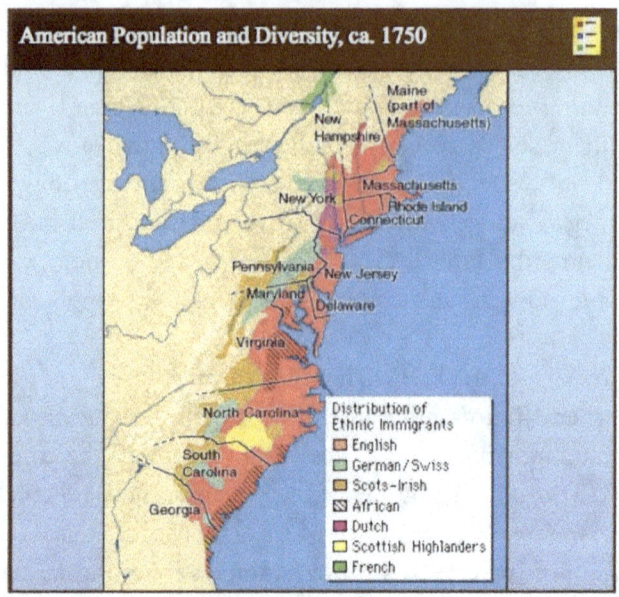

Map and Data from University of Oregon at
MappingHistory.UOregon.edu/english/US/US04-02.html

The above map shows major concentrations of ethnic and racial groups living in British North America in the middle of the eighteenth century. In addition to the major concentrations shown here, numerous other pockets of diversity existed throughout the English colonies, such as Iberian Jewish communities in Rhode Island and Swedish farming districts in New Jersey. Many of these diverse groups still spoke their native languages.

The vast majority of European ethnic groups came to the English colonies voluntarily, while some of the first residents from Africa made the long and dangerous trip more-or-less voluntarily as indentured freemen servants in the early 1600s. Freemen had several civil rights that faded away as involuntary slave laborers starting entering the colonies in the mid 1600s. Though heavily concentrated in a few regions, Africans and their progeny eventually comprised roughly one-fifth of America's total population as demand for hard physical labor grew during the 1700s. Native American enclaves also remained interspersed among the European settlements in many areas during those eras.

The History and Culture of Coalfields Southwest Virginia

The Cherokee initially helped the British and their American colonial militias take up arms against the French and their northern tribal allies. These alliances were complex because some Native American tribes fought for whoever provided them with firepower, whiskey, and flattery, while others fought Whites of all nationalities. Many of the tribes had killed each other for centuries—even thousands of years—and those long-held grudges were oftentimes more fierce than the fear of the Whites invading their territories. So it was not too surprising that in 1758 the Cherokee and English-speaking White settlers carved out a separate war among themselves, called the Anglo-Cherokee War, as each side accused the other of treachery and broken promises.

French forces were vastly outnumbered by American militias and the relatively few English troops that assisted them in the American interior. England also had superior naval forces and, as a result of those advantages, that country was victorious over the French and Indian allies in 1763. That war then spread to the European Theater and was known as the Seven Years War, but the "French and Indian War" remained the name of the American struggle within the emerging English colonies.

To appreciate Virginia's major role in this and subsequent wars, readers should understand the ever-evolving size and shape of the Mother State. The following maps illustrate geographical Virginia and its borders leading up to the French and Indian War, the Revolutionary War, the eventual adoption of the U.S. Constitution, and beyond.

In order to obtain the votes to ratify the U.S. Constitution, Virginia had to make territorial concessions to smaller and sometimes landlocked states. These states rightfully feared that their huge geographical neighbor would dominate and likely monopolize the future growth of the new nation. To finalize the state's frequent border changes, the last map below is the Old Dominion's current boundaries after West Virginia became a separate state in 1863. The nation's 35th state is the only one formed by the federal government from another state's territory against the host's wishes.

The following maps of Virginia over the centuries (left to right) were commissioned for this book and prepared by Karl Phillips of

Leesburg, Virginia. **The text history of each of these maps can be found at www.CoalfieldsPublishing.com/VirginiaBoundaries for readers who are particularly interested in details as to how Virginia and America got where they are today, geographically and politically.**

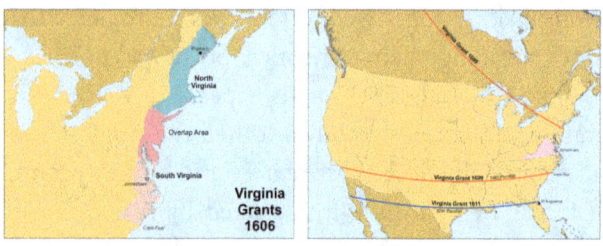

Virginia Boundaries 1608 and 1611

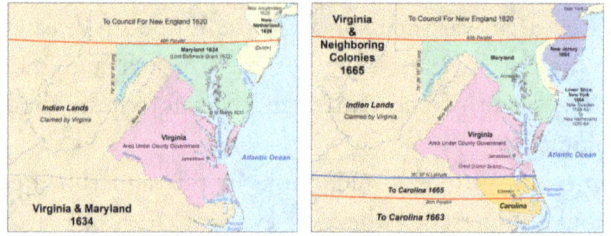

Virginia Boundaries 1634 and 1655

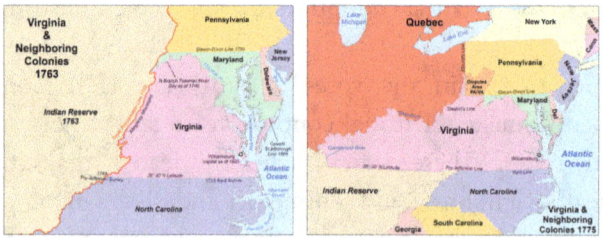

Virginia Boundaries 1763 and 1775

The History and Culture of Coalfields Southwest Virginia

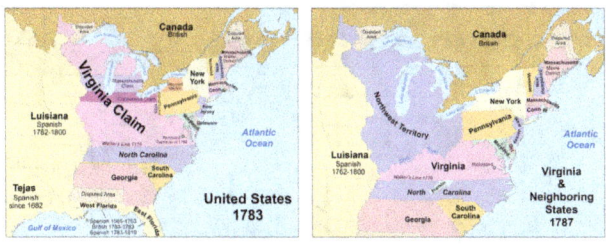

Virginia Boundaries 1783 and 1787

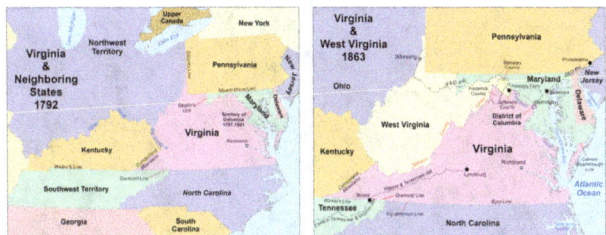

Virginia Boundaries 1792 and 1863

The French and Indian War ended in 1763, the same year England's King George III signed a proclamation forbidding new settlers from crossing the Blue Ridge Mountains, including far Southwest Virginia, into what was then considered Cherokee hunting grounds. Unfortunately for the King and Native residents, a few thousand White settlers had already crossed that line, and the King's proclamation had no effect other than to add one more grievance against England by its White subjects from Scotland, Ireland, Wales, Germany, and the most land hungry of them all, the Scots-Irish. Scottish subjects of the King who ended up on the wrong side of frequent wars to seat a new monarch were frequently forced into Northern Ireland as exiles in a vain attempt to subdue the Irish Celtic warrior blood.

King George III's Proclamation Line, signed in 1763

Although kin by DNA, the two groups of Celtic people were divided by religion (Irish Catholics versus Scottish Protestants), cultures, and tribal instincts. The displaced Scots were never fully accepted by the native Irish, and so the resulting Scots/Irish families were bereft of land, good jobs, and hopeful futures. Accordingly, by the tens of thousands they boarded the many ships heading west to America in the mid-1700s, and found Appalachia to be a place where the mountain terrain was familiar, the land was free or nearly so, and the freedom of movement, religion, and occupations of choice were relatively unfettered.

Just prior to this great exodus, the Ohio Company employed noted surveyor Christopher Gist to accompany an expedition of Englishmen to explore and map land in the Ohio River region and other east-side tributaries of the Mississippi. Some historians believe that Gist, in October of 1750, traveled on horseback to the Cumberland Mountains at Pounds Gap, wandered east to a prominent plateau (present day Wise, Virginia), then turned down Gist's River (now

Guest) and made it all the way to the Clinch River. The modern Commonwealth of Virginia ends within miles of Gist's turnaround point near Cumberland Gap. However, the colony of eighteenth-century Virginia did not stop there, and she claimed all lands westward to the Mississippi River. A variety of land companies favored by the King gobbled up new lands, sometimes sight unseen, and became very prosperous by selling off these holdings to other speculators and land-hungry immigrants and their progeny. The King forgot his father's promise to his Native American guests once he realized his orders were being defied and the Indian lands were very valuable.

Surveyor Christopher Gist, Artwork by Darris Stanley

Meanwhile, American militia veterans of the French and Indian War received land grants from Virginia in sizes of 50 to 5,000 acres. The European-bred newcomers were certainly not leaving the Appalachians as commanded by the King; in fact, more came every day. The Native American tribes claiming the same lands, in particular the Cherokee, felt betrayed and abandoned, and reacted as any people protecting their land and families would against an invading force; they fought bravely and savagely against what turned out to be impossible odds. The Indian Wars that arose in far Southwest Virginia from the 1750s—when trappers and a few desperate settlers first arrived—and lasted until almost 1800 were not very pretty. Both sides exacted murderous atrocities upon the other.

Typical Ancient Cherokee Village in What Is Now North Carolina, courtesy of www.NativeVillage.org

The Shawnee gladly sided with French soldiers residing in the Ohio River Valley and waged war on settlers throughout Southwest Virginia before, during, and after the French and Indian War. Later, during the Revolutionary War, the tribe sided with the English and attacked White settlers throughout the region. Hundreds, if not thousands, of settlers were shot by bow and gun, stabbed, tomahawked, burned, and tortured to death. Even more Native Americans died from similar tactics employed by the settlers and their militias.

After England won the French and Indian War and the Native Americans were on their own, all-out war ensued. The constant battles increased in the 1770s when a long string of militia-controlled forts was established along the east banks of the Clinch River, which flows southwesterly from cave springs in present day Tazewell County, Virginia, to the French Broad River in what is now Tennessee.

The Virginia forts were mostly blockhouses made of logs with windows narrow enough that attackers could not climb through, yet wide enough that defenders could poke their musket barrels outside to unleash hot lead. These defensive structures were quickly built at intervals of ten to twenty miles so that settlers were never more than a daylight horseback ride from fort to fort. The most intact fort remaining today is Kilgore Fort in Scott County, Virginia, erected by my ancestors in the late 1700s.

The well-preserved Kilgore Fort is shown below.

A replica of a block house fort located at the remarkable Crab Orchard Museum near Tazewell, Virginia. Note the portals used to shoot from, but not be shot

The largest and most well-known of those forts was named Moore's Fort, in what was then called Castle's Woods (now Castlewood) in present-day Russell County. This pioneer community was named after its founder, Jacob Cassell, the son of a German immigrant. He was reported to have "bought" that entire area from a Native American for a musket and butcher knife.

Jacob Cassell bartering with a skeptical native, artwork by Darris Stanley

Long Hunters Jacob Cassell and William Clinch, 1760s Clinch was the namesake of the Clinch River and Clinch Mountain. Artwork by Jeff Goodson

JACOB ALLEGEDLY TOOK on more than one Cherokee bride, which may explain the widely held legend and absolute belief that half or so of Far Southwest Virginia's population is of Cherokee descent. I cannot count the times that hundreds of my friends and family have stated with certainty that their grandmother or great-grandmother was "full-blooded or half-blooded" Cherokee. DNA testing has debunked that legend, but the local oral history supporting this myth will not soon die. Even a former presidential candidate, Elizabeth Warren, believed her family's similar generational stories about having significant Oklahoma Cherokee genes in her veins. She was challenged to take a DNA test and the results were powerfully weak. Hopefully it is flattering to the present-day Cherokee people that so many Whites yearn to be related to them, but somehow I doubt it.

CHAPTER 14
MOORE'S FORT IN CASTLE'S WOODS CIRCA 1774

Moore's Fort was an acre or so in size and held a garrison of over a hundred well-armed soldiers and spies. They and their families resided in what was likely the only palisade fort of its kind along the river. Descriptions of the fort are based upon old records and witness accounts. The exact location of the fort, now rotted into history, is being researched and pursued by me and other curious students of local history. The artist's rendition of the fort below is based, as much as possible, upon the various accounts available.

Moore's Fort in Castle's Woods, circa 1774

The History and Culture of Coalfields Southwest Virginia

None other than *the* Daniel Boone was the militia captain of Moore's Fort from 1773 to 1775, just prior to his successful settlers' trek through the Cumberland Gap to present-day Eastern Kentucky. His first visit to the "Dark and Bloody Ground" is said to have been June 7, 1769 while on a "long hunt," so named because the trappers and explorers of the time were called "long hunters" by the Natives. It is still debated if that name was due to the long treks taken by these rugged men, or because the Native Americans opined that they had stayed in their territory "too long." Another theory, proffered by this book's editor, is that the Native Americans were referring to the long rifles used by these trappers, which actually sounds more logical than the older theories.

Moore's Fort was struck three times in September of 1774 by Chief Logan and his Mingoes. The Mingo Tribe had a strong presence in what is now southern West Virginia. Chief Logan, whose father was French, was out to avenge the absolute murder of his entire family by what he thought were rogue militia members. Later it was determined that local settlers posing as militia members killed the Mingo chief's family for their own revengeful purposes.

Though very brave, yet reckless in their attempts, the Mingo warriors were unable to inflict any casualties or capture any prisoners until the third attack on September 29. By then, aware that it was pointless to openly charge the fort, Chief Logan waited patiently in the surrounding forests until the inhabitants within those walls thought all was safe. His tactic was partly successful, and the chief left behind Cherokee war clubs so the fort defenders and militias bound to chase the killers would not realize it was Logan. The Mingoes were ultimately subdued and Logan, a very eloquent leader and thinker, sent a letter to Virginia's Governor Dunmore after his revenge was spent. The text of his letter is haunting.

> A Colonel Creasp the last spring (1774), in cold blood and unprovoked, murdered all the relations of Logan, not even sparing my women and children. There runs not a drop of my blood in any living creature. This called on me for revenge. I have sought it. I have killed many. I have glutted my vengeance.

Chief Logan's sorrow is illustrated in a book published in 1854 entitled *The Captives of Abb's Valley,* a story touched upon later in this book.

"WHO IS THERE TO MOURN FOR LOGAN? NOT ONE."

Editor's Note: Historians differ on whether or not a British colonial flag (which differs from the Union Jack) would have been flown on the series of forts along the Clinch River. Moore's Fort being the largest, it seems logical that it would have raised the flag if any such fort did. Since anti-king sentiments were strong west of the Blue Ridge leading up to the building of the forts, most militia leaders probably raised the flag only if Virginia's colonial governor made it part of funding construction. This painting by Jeff Goodson of St. Paul, Virginia, includes the British colonial flag for historic effect, if not for accuracy.

The History and Culture of Coalfields Southwest Virginia

Chief Logan—like many Native Americans, particularly chieftains—was eloquent and wise, even in defeat. Shawnee Chief Tecumseh, below, rendered his philosophy of life after years of battles, woes, and setbacks.

So live your life that the fear of death can never enter your heart. Trouble no one about their religion; respect others in their view, and demand that they respect yours. Love your life, perfect your life, beautify all things in your life. Seek to make your life long and its purpose in the service of your people. Prepare a noble death song for the day when you go over the great divide. Always give a word or a sign of salute when meeting or passing a friend, even a stranger, when in a lonely place. Show respect to all people and grovel to none. When you arise in the morning give thanks for the food and for the joy of living. If you see no reason for giving thanks, the fault lies only in yourself. Abuse no one and no thing, for abuse turns the wise ones to fools and robs the spirit of its vision. When it comes your time to die, be not like those whose hearts are filled with the fear of death, so that when their time comes they weep and pray for a little more time to live their lives over again in a different way. Sing your death song and die like a hero going home.

Chief Tecumseh, Shawnee Nation (NOTE: Tecumseh was raised in present day Ohio along with several White foster brothers, captives from many raids).

After these Mingo attacks were repelled, Boone was even more determined to settle that vast western wilderness named Kentucky. He recruited settlers who were not content to remain on the east side of Cumberland Mountain (also known as Pine Mountain in the northern sector). His first attempt, in October of 1773, was marred by the killing of his son, James Boone, and Henry Russell, the son of Boone's venture partner, William Russell. A multi-tribe band of assassins made up of mostly Delaware braves, along with Shawnee and Cherokee interpreters and Cherokee Chief Big Elk, waylaid and tortured the young men in a most merciless fashion near Wallen's Ridge in today's Lee County. The skinning and burning of the boys was typical for those times, and both fathers had to be paralyzed with grief, and motivated even more by hatred.

Boone retreated to Moore's Fort and gathered his physical and emotional strength for the next, and successful, trek to Kentucky in 1775. There he established a small community named Boone's Station, later renamed Fort Boonesborough. He also worked for the Transylvania Company, which partly explains his lust for moving ever westward. His boss, Richard Henderson, ran afoul of the Virginia colony and English investors when he tried to form a new colony named Transylvania. In June of 1776, just prior to proclaiming its independence from England, the Virginia House of Burgesses (the New World's oldest European legislative body, circa 1619) prohibited the new colony which became the state of Kentucky in 1792. Ironically, Boone was elected to the Virginia state legislature while Kentucky was a mere county of the state. Just imagine his arduous trips by horseback and foot to and from Richmond and the wilderness he represented.

The History and Culture of Coalfields Southwest Virginia

Historians differ over Clinch's first name but the dates William explored west of the New River, starting in 1742, are in the range of later years when the earliest pioneers emerged into what is now the Clinch Valley. Historians agree that the Clinch River and Clinch Mountain were named after a Clinch, which was likely William, but that is not settled. Interestingly, a William Clinch was expelled from the Virginia House of Burgesses in 1757. He was reelected in 1758 but was not allowed to serve and the election was held again. Other historians make the case that it was Jeremiah Clinch that associated with Daniel Boone as a long hunter in the Greater Holston Valley which neighbors the Clinch Valley. This also is compelling because Clinch Mountain sheds rain east and west into both valleys.

Few people know that Daniel Boone was a member of the Virginia legislature for three terms. At the start of the Revolutionary War, Kentucky was a huge county of the Old Dominion, and slowly other counties were established as more and more people staked claims there. Boone's last term of office was 1791, one year before Kentucky became the nation's 15th state. After losing money in a variety of endeavors, he died a pauper. But his legend was and still is that of a pioneering icon.

Daniel Boone Escorting Settlers through the Cumberland Gap (George Caleb Bingham, oil on canvas, 1851–52)

During the Revolutionary War, Boone helped defend his own fort against English-led Shawnee in 1778. The English whipped up the Natives against American settlers in an attempt to stop the Revolution. That tactic backfired when Appalachian militias burned to the ground several Native American towns and villages from the Ohio Valley to the Cherokee lands south of Virginia. The Native Americans suffered terribly, and many eventually died from starvation and exposure as White militias raided numerous Cherokee and Shawnee towns and burned or carried away their winter food caches. It was all-out war that lasted a very long time.

Some of these same militiamen, including a dozen or so of my ancestors, helped turn the tide of the Revolutionary War at the Battle of King's Mountain in October of 1780. A few months later, a joint effort of American regular troops, local militiamen, and Indian fighters (including some King's Mountain veterans) continued the Patriots' winning streak. This second showdown, named the Battle of Cowpens, also took place in northern South Carolina, with similar results. The main difference between the two fights is that at Cowpens, Cornwallis unleashed his best English soldiers and a few Tories in his command to break the back and will of the South. He evidently believed that his well-trained Redcoats could do what the all-Tory army at King's Mountain could not. These combined losses ran the British northward, as discussed later in this book.

The most infamous massacre by Native Americans in far Southwest Virginia involved James Moore and his family in Abb's Valley, a beautiful hand-cleared farm settlement in today's Tazewell County. Chief Black Wolf of the Shawnee Nation killed and/or captured the entire family in 1786, having previously kidnapped the eldest son, James, Jr., in 1784. This string of massacres and the kidnappings of the patriarch's wife, son, and daughters are as suspenseful as a horror story can be. Below is the original text from the Virginia State Papers of the time, which recorded field notes of the Moore family massacre. Walter Crockett, County Lieutenant of Montgomery Co., wrote to Governor Patrick Henry, on July 21, 1786, (1) saying:

> I am sorry to inform your Excellency that on the 14th instant, a party of Indians supposed to be about 40 or 50 in number, came to the house of Captain James Moore on Bluestone, in this county, and killed himself, and his whole family, eleven in number, and carried off his whole stock, which was very valuable. They likewise burned the house and fencing, and left several war clubs and arrows, and to all appurtenances are for continuing hostilities.

Another letter written by Alexander Barnett, County Lieutenant of Russell Co., to the Governor, dated August 12, 1786, (2) states:

> The late attempt of the Indians on Bluestone, when destroying Captain Moore's family (which I expect you have been informed of), from the best account I can get, was the Cherokees, and not exceeding 10 or 12 in number. Upon receiving report of it, I issued orders to send out spies, three pair, one for the upper part of the county; one for the center, and one for the lower end. The two in the center that went from Castle's Woods discovered a trace of moccasin tracks and horses that had sometime before traveled along the top of Cumberland Mountain. They reported they followed them about 10

miles, still on the Cumberland Mountain. They say the Indians, as they suspect them to be, had about 7 or 8 horses, and 4 or 5 on foot. It is assumed that they are the same that was at Moore's on Bluestone, as it appears that is the number of horses taken from there at that time.

1. Virginia State Papers, Vol. IV, page 159.
2. Virginia State Papers, Vol. IV, page 163.

Black Wolf and captive James Moore Jr., artwork by Darris Stanley

James Moore, Jr., below, praying after his capture, and his captive sister, Polly, reading her Bible to a protective inferior chieftain. He was intrigued by her reading written words from a book, as illustrated here from *The Captives of Abb's Valley: A Legend of Frontier Life, 1854.*

The History and Culture of Coalfields Southwest Virginia

"James kneeled down and engaged in prayer to God."

"He often called her to read to him out of her New Testament."

Moore Family Massacre, artwork by Darris Stanley

If the Cherokee hated any people more than they despised White settlers, it was the Shawnee. The two warring tribes took a timeout from scalping White settlers and burning down their cabins long enough to fight their most fierce, and last, toe-to-toe battle.

Whether the Xualans were displaced and destroyed a century earlier by Spanish diseases, by enemy tribes, or both, the Cherokee were now under full assault by White militias. During the period of 1760-90, the more aggressive chiefs and warriors of this very militant tribe frequently went north from their towns (in present day Tennessee and North Carolina) to fight the Southwest Virginia settlers hand-to-hand and cabin-to-cabin. The Shawnee would craftily pick times when the Cherokee or the settlers had been disrupted and weakened by each other to attack the survivors. Brilliant, upon reflection.

This was the situation as the ultimate battle between the two tribes started to unfold near the foot of Rich Mountain in present day Tazewell County. The year was 1768, and the first White settlers had not been in the region very long and were routinely attacked by both tribes.

When a Shawnee hunting party of about 200 braves unexpectedly came upon a Cherokee party of approximately the same number, the standoff soon erupted into a rare, set battle amongst them.

Shawnee scouts prepping for the battle, artwork by Darris Stanley

The Cherokee entrenched at the top of Rich Mountain and actually dug a defensive perimeter, a rare tactic for such mobile Native warriors. The Shawnee attacked that very evening, then withdrew at dusk only to return the next morning for an all-day fight to the death. The nearby White settlers cynically supplied both tribes with lead and gunpowder and, for once, were bystanders. The battle carried over to the next day, but the Shawnee finally surrendered and the survivors jointly buried their dead in a large common grave.

For the next year or so, the Cherokee remained the dominant tribe in the region and tolerated the presence of other tribes passing through or hunting game so they could focus upon the relentless westward push by settlers. In a major tactical error, the Cherokee, likely pumped up due to their recent victory over the Shawnee, tried in 1769 to wipe out the Chickasaw tribe to their west and failed miserably, thereby weakening their forces.

The French and Indian War against the settlers ended in 1763, and there was no sustained, coordinated effort afterwards by the Native American tribes in the southern region to take on the next wave of White immigrants. Slowly but surely, the Cherokee were driven back south to their towns, and they established more isolated, defendable communities, only to be burned out and killed by a variety of state militias.

The tribal elders wanted peace and the end of the killings, but many of the younger warriors demanded revenge, and the pursuit of that passion caused even more overwhelming retaliations. Young and passionate Chief Dragging Canoe, along with scores of like-minded braves and their families, went as far as to leave the original Cherokee Nation to continue a fierce resistance to White intrusions. The new tribe was called the Chickamauga (or Lower Cherokee because of the tribe's new location), and a whole new series of attacks on White settlements ensued. Although militia leaders knew the Cherokee elders and their fighters were not involved in the multi-tribe retaliations, the governing bodies of the affected states gathered overpowering, well-armed, crack-shot forces to indiscriminately annihilate Cherokee towns and villages. Dragging Canoe, not one to say "uncle," sided with the English during the Revolutionary War, only to return to his new village to find it completely destroyed.

Cherokee Holocaust, artwork by Darris Stanley

After Dragging Canoe announced his cynicism about the true intentions of the White settlers to destroy and displace his people, his militant actions certainly sped up that process. But as history proved, his predictions came true regardless of his elders' concessions or his occasional battle victories.

Chief Dragging Canoe, artwork by Darris Stanley

CHAPTER 15
THE REVOLUTIONARY WAR IN THE MOUNTAINS

IN ADDITION to some Native American tribes siding with the English in Appalachia, there were also fierce battles among Americans in that so-called Seven Year War. The Americans loyal to the King were dubbed "Tories" (or Loyalists), and the pro-revolution Americans called themselves Patriots.

As mentioned previously, an October, 1780 seminal battle fought in the extreme northern area of South Carolina, called the Battle of King's Mountain, literally turned the tide of the war for American independence.

England's General Cornwallis and his highly trained army and naval forces headquartered at Charleston were occupying South Carolina, having already subjugated Georgia, and were on the cusp of overtaking North Carolina. Cornwallis planned to then attack Virginia from the south, while other Redcoat forces pushed southward from northern strongholds. English military leaders foresaw no American forces that could stop these steamroller advances after the epic surrender of thousands of Patriot soldiers at Charleston. If the South fell, the war would be practically impossible for the new nation to win. George Washington's goal of freedom was very much in question.

In October of 1780, a Redcoat Major, Patrick Ferguson, made the mistake of sending a threatening message to the hunters, trappers, and

Indian fighters who had settled along the southern Appalachian frontiers, including what is now Southwest Virginia. His dire warning was that if they continued to interrupt the English takeover of North Carolina, death and destruction awaited (as displayed by the National Park Service's "Abingdon Muster Grounds" in Washington County, Virginia).

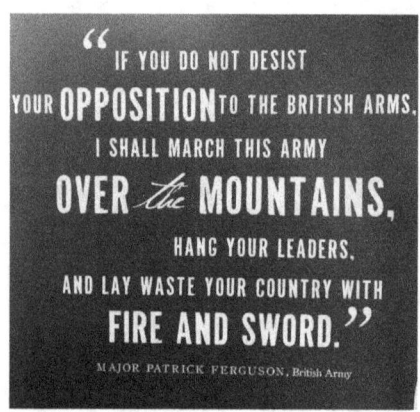

Instead of waiting for Ferguson and his army of Tories to carry out his mission, the mostly Scots-Irish militias from the mountains of Virginia and North Carolina mustered over 1,400 crack-shot fighters to track down and kill the arrogant Scottish officer and as many Tories as possible. A small contingent of South Carolinians gladly joined the fray in retaliation of Ferguson's role in killing hundreds, if not thousands, of lowland Patriots and their families. To make things worse for the Tories, an English officer (Tarleton) had, in a prior skirmish, refused to recognize the white-flag surrender of defeated Patriots, and many of them, including their wounded, were shot or bayoneted. That was not forgotten.

Overmountain Men Looking for a Fight, artwork by Darris Stanley

Using guerrilla tactics learned the hard way from battle-tested Native Americans, the French and Indian War, and prior lesser battles against Tories, the men who crossed over the mountains looking for a fight were dubbed the "Overmountain Men." The opposing army of pro-England Americans was of a similar number, and having the high ground made them very confident as they listened to the crowing of their cocky Scottish military leader. Both armies held back reserves and base-camp attendants, so the actual battle numbers were approximately 1,000 men for each side. Not a big battle in modern terms, but considered sizable forces in the days of our sparsely populated colonies, especially in the mountains.

The Tories were gathered in a defensive position on top of a low-profile hill, ironically named King's Mountain. Their major decided they did not need to entrench to beat a bunch of "illiterate backwoodsmen." The Patriots used every rock and tree as cover, and employed evasive tactics learned from years of rough-terrain battles. They also possessed the world's most accurate rifles, made by Pennsylvania German gunsmiths. These gifted gun makers used the fairly new technology of rifled barrels as opposed to the smooth-barreled muskets used by the English forces and Washington's troops. As it turns out, many of these so-called illiterate backwoodsmen made handsome incomes from fur trading and therefore could afford the world's best rifles, which were literally their tools of trade and survival.

The Overmountain Men then commenced surrounding and

slaughtering hundreds of Tories. Legend has it that Major Ferguson was shot seven times before he became dislodged from his white war horse and fell to the ground to be finished off.

The final lopsided tally is hard to fathom: 290 Tories killed, 163 wounded, and the rest captured, compared to twenty-eight Patriot deaths and sixty wounded. The battle was difficult to stop even with Tory white flags of surrender popping up. Eventually the Patriots ceased fire and hastened back to their mountain redoubts. Along the way, some of the Tory prisoners were "tried" for what we would today call war crimes, and were hanged or shot on the spot.

Thomas Jefferson reminisced in his later years that this key battle "was the joyful annunciation of that turn of the tide of success which terminated the revolutionary war, with the seal of our independence." Theodore Roosevelt wrote, "This brilliant victory marked the turning point of the American Revolution." Herbert Hoover went even further as he stood at King's Mountain: "This small band of patriots turned back a dangerous invasion well designed to separate and dismember the united colonies. It was a little army and a little battle but it was of mighty portent. **History has done scant justice to its significance, which should rightly place it beside Lexington, Bunker Hill, Trenton and Yorktown."** And get this, Sir Henry Clinton, the British Commander-in-Chief of the Crown's North America war efforts, had this to say about King's Mountain: "…an event which was immediately productive of the worst consequences to the King's affairs in South Carolina, and unhappily proved the first link of a Chain of Evils that followed each other in regular succession until they at last ended in the total loss of America."

In less eloquent words, the Overmountain Men overwhelmingly kicked the rears of English forces and caused a ripple effect that won the war.

This battle was the first major Patriot victory to occur after the British invasion of the South. Cornwallis became so paranoid of these and other backwoods killers that he temporarily fortified himself and other military brass against a possible attack on Charleston. One could say that the Overmountain Men were comparable to the Navy Seals of today, given their toughness and deadly fighting skills.

The History and Culture of Coalfields Southwest Virginia

AUTHOR'S NOTE: Like most humans, Major Ferguson was not all bad. In 1777, while serving as a young British captain in Pennsylvania, Ferguson—a storied marksman—spied an American officer on horseback with few Patriots in sight. Ferguson aimed his rifle, which he had designed, at the stoic officer who simply glanced at him and slowly moved on. The Scotsman decided not to shoot the American officer in the back. "I could have lodged half a dozen balls in or about him, before he was out of my reach," Ferguson recalled, "but it was not pleasant to fire at the back of an unoffending individual, who was acquitting himself very coolly of his duty—so I let him alone." Afterwards he learned that the individual was likely George Washington, the future first president of the United States.

Don Troiani's description - "Colonel Cleveland's War Prize Oct. 7, 1780." Col. Benjamin Cleveland returning to Wilkesboro on Patrick Ferguson's white horse after his horse, Roebuck, and Ferguson were killed. The patriots took home drums, weapons and clothes. The other colonels awarded Cleveland with Ferguson's white horse, which he rode home. Many consider this the greatest symbolic "War Prize" of the revolution and the turning point of the war. (These and other Troiana renditions are available online at www.WBritain.com)

The kiosk photos below were taken at the Keller Interpretive Center at the Abingdon Muster Grounds site in Southwest Virginia. The site is part of the Overmountain Victory National Historic Trail, passing 330 miles through four states. At the time of this battle, Washington County encompassed all of what is now far Southwest Virginia.

> *At* 3:00 p.m. on October 7th, the patriot militia army finally caught up with Ferguson and his men. Nine hundred patriots turned their rifles against Ferguson's one thousand one hundred musket-bearing loyalists. After a fierce one-hour and five minute battle, all loyalists troops were dead, wounded, or captured, compared to fewer than 100 patriot casualties. The positions on the mountain and weaponry proved to greatly benefit the patriots. Ferguson was shot dead during the battle, leaving Cornwallis without a suitable leader for the vital frontier, and consequently keeping North Carolina and Virginia out of British control.
>
> ABINGDON MUSTER GROUNDS, VIRGINIA
> *The Virginia patriot militia departed from Abingdon, Virginia on September 24, 1780. There were approximately 400 men and horses from this area.*

AUTHOR'S NOTE: The National Park Service confirms above that the Battle of King's Mountain kept North Carolina and Virginia out of British control.

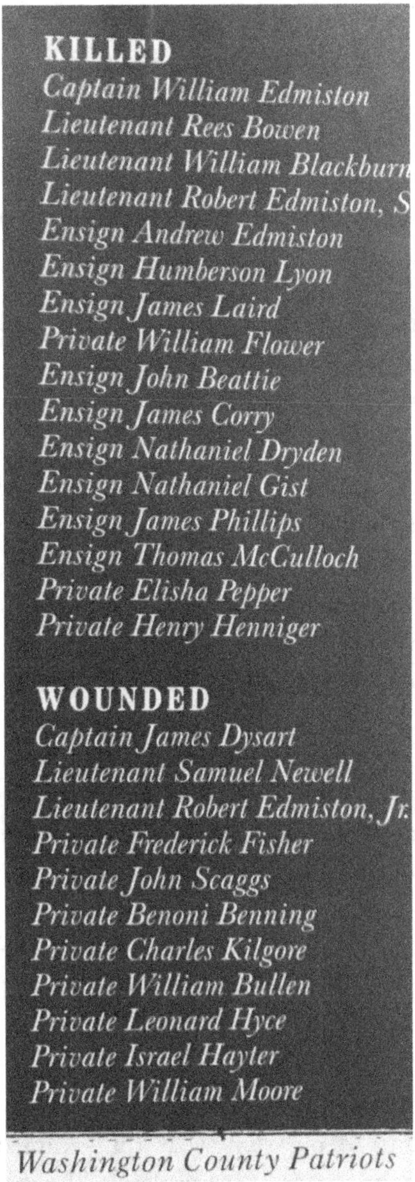

KILLED
Captain William Edmiston
Lieutenant Rees Bowen
Lieutenant William Blackburn
Lieutenant Robert Edmiston, S
Ensign Andrew Edmiston
Ensign Humberson Lyon
Ensign James Laird
Private William Flower
Ensign John Beattie
Ensign James Corry
Ensign Nathaniel Dryden
Ensign Nathaniel Gist
Ensign James Phillips
Ensign Thomas McCulloch
Private Elisha Pepper
Private Henry Henniger

WOUNDED
Captain James Dysart
Lieutenant Samuel Newell
Lieutenant Robert Edmiston, Jr.
Private Frederick Fisher
Private John Scaggs
Private Benoni Benning
Private Charles Kilgore
Private William Bullen
Private Leonard Hyce
Private Israel Hayter
Private William Moore

Washington County Patriots

Washington County Patriots killed and wounded at Kings Mountain. This photo was taken at the Keller Interpretive Center at the Abingdon Muster Grounds site. The site is part of the Overmountain Victory National Historic Trail, passing 330 miles through four states.

In January of the next year, 300 regular American soldiers, along with 740 Virginian and other frontier militiamen, decisively defeated English forces at the Battle of Cowpens in South Carolina, about forty miles from King's Mountain. The Patriots, led by General Daniel Morgan, borrowed tactics from the King's Mountain playbook that included strategic retreats, which led to ambushing opponents by way of flanking the enemy at the precise time to maximize confusion and slaughter among the enemy forces. All in all, 800 of Lt. Colonel Tarleton's 1,000 Redcoat soldiers were killed or captured. Tarleton, a very arrogant and sadistic military commander, was last seen riding his high horse as fast as he could in full retreat as his men lay dead, wounded, or captured.

Morgan's battle tactics were much superior to the straight-ahead English assault. He pulled off a rarely executed "double envelopment," which is a pincer movement that attacks both of the enemy's flanks at the same time. As a primer, the Overmountain Men executed a daring 360-degree multi-flank attack as they advanced up King's Mountain from all directions. Morgan lost only twenty-five men and only 124 were wounded.

By a long shot, the new country's ragtag soldiers and hickory-tough backwoodsmen annihilated the world's best-trained and -tried soldiers of that time. Together the Appalachians racked up a 10:1 kill ratio at King's Mountain, and a mix of regular and mountain troops achieved a 4:1 ratio at Cowpens. Morgan also took hundreds of British soldiers off the field of combat as prisoners; literally the two battles took away nearly half of Cornwallis' original ground invasion forces by death, serious wounds, and capture.

And this was not Morgan's first encounter with the British. He was previously a wagoner for the Redcoats in the war against the French and Indians. Being somewhat thin-skinned, this American gladiator took great umbrage at being slapped by the broad side of an English officer's sword. After knocking his superior out with one punch, Morgan received 499 lashes (the flogger miscounted the 500 ordered licks), nearly killing him. Apparently Morgan did have thin skin, plus hundreds of scars and a long memory, so the Revolutionary War gave him a chance to prove just how irritated he was. Prior to

The History and Culture of Coalfields Southwest Virginia

Cowpens, www.Battlefields.org gives Morgan this praise (paraphrased by this author): "He marched a company of crack riflemen from Virginia to New England in just twenty-one days. His southern forces gained a reputation for fighting hard and shooting straight. The British Regulars were intimidated by these killers dressed in hunting shirts."

But Morgan's earlier southern foray into northern battlegrounds was just a whiff of what was to come home to the English.

General Cornwallis subsequently won a lesser battle against the Patriots at Greensboro, North Carolina, but took on so many casualties among his dwindling army that he had to abandon the South. That is called a defeat and a retreat in all reputable history circles except for one, as mentioned in the next chapter.

The spiffy Redcoat commander had lost too much (more than half of his initial southern ground troop forces were dead, permanently injured, or captured), so he mustered his survivors to chase elusive Patriot units northward. He then, in a rare smart decision, gave up any idea of recapturing the South. Rather, he pushed his beleaguered troops toward their eventual beatdown and surrender at Yorktown, Virginia.

Ironically, Cornwallis' defeat and surrender to General Washington on October, 19, 1781, was almost one year to the day after the Tories' severe defeat at King's Mountain. These southern victories were very timely; Washington's northern forces during years 1779 through early 1781 were mostly unpaid, malnourished, despondent, and suffering freezing conditions, which caused many of his troops to desert and, even worse, participate in at least three organized mutinies. After some of the mutinous ringleaders were captured, Washington commanded their own comrades to kill them via firing squad, while other select leaders of the sustained insurrections were hanged. In other words, the Revolution was in deep peril until insulted Appalachians got involved. Think it through. While Washington was reduced to killing his own desperate men, mountain Patriots were mowing down Tories and Redcoats.

Below are the final statistics for the entire eight-year war for both sides, provided by www.RevolutionaryWar.us:

AMERICAN CASUALTIES:
- Total Combat Killed and Wounded = 10,683
- Total Combat and non-Combat Deaths = 25,324
- Total Combat and non-Combat Wounded = 8,44

BRITISH CASUALTIES:
- Army: 43,633 total dead = 9,372 killed in battle, 27,000 died of disease
- Navy: 1,243 killed in battle, 18,500 died of disease (1776–1780), 42,000 deserted
- Loyalists: 7,000 total dead, 1,700 killed in battle, 5,300 died of disease (estimated)
- Germans: 7,774 total dead, 1,800 killed in battle, 4,888 deserted

(NOTE: These numbers seem very low stacked against modern wars, but the American population was only 2.78 million as of 1780, many of whom (fifteen to twenty percent) were British Loyalists. Also note the German mercenary desertions; many of these runaways settled in Appalachia for sanctuary and became solid mountain residents. The English Navy obviously had a struggle with fleeing naval soldiers as well, who blended into the more coastal areas.)

CHAPTER 16
THE HISTORY CHANNEL INSULTS ALL APPALACHIANS AND THEIR ANCESTORS

It is worth re-emphasizing that the Revolutionary War in the South, and the participation of Appalachian patriots in winning that struggle, has been purposely ignored. This enormous pre-meditated slight toward Appalachians requires a remedy. By warping history to its liking, the History Channel insults all Appalachians and our ancestors. Its series about the Revolutionary War carries nary a peep about the Battle of King's Mountain and how it paved the way for future non-traditional battle strategies that subdued the Tories and ultimately drove the British from the South.

These southern victories literally cleared the way for our fledgling nation to win the War of Independence. This is particularly evident by the fact that the entire American southern army was killed or captured in and around Charleston just months before the Overmountain Men swooped down to save the day.

Just as today, Appalachian military heroes are the Rodney Dangerfields of America (For younger readers, this iconic comedian made millions saying "I don't get no respect," so check him out on YouTube).

Here is the clear and convincing proof against a very biased history source. In the award-winning series *Washington*, the History Channel had this to say about Cornwallis: "General Charles Cornwallis, who spent most of the last two years in the Carolinas, is now *moving* to Virginia. General Cornwallis is one of the *ablest* British generals, is quick-minded, he moves aggressively (and) knows how to handle troops in the field. Lord Cornwallis 'DECIDED' to go to Virginia."

Then the program's narrator goes on to deep-dive into Cornwallis's wigged, snow-white head and came up with this quote he divined that the British faux juggernaut was likely musing: "Virginia is home to Washington, home to Jefferson, all those patriot leaders. If I can make them suffer maybe I can get the Patriots to come to terms."

Somebody please gift the History Channel bigwigs with a Google account. They portray Cornwallis as a worthy adversary and brilliant military leader when, in fact, he was beaten like a drum as he ventured north toward the North Carolina and Virginia mountains.

According to these dubious history experts, this stuffy, overrated English military leader rose from his plush bed one fine day, draped himself in a silk leisure robe, looked around and said to his attaché, "My work here is done; I have conquered everything in my sight, except for a few barbarians from the mountains, and so it is I shall leave on my own accord, in a daring fashion, and finish off the American riffraff at Yorktown."

Once again, a biased media and some highly credentialed erstwhile "historians" simply will not give credit to the South, much less Appalachians, for literally saving the all-but-defeated American cause.

In two masterful battles at the upper reaches of South Carolina, George Washington went from almost certain defeat in the North (as his troops struggled to survive) to an ultimate victory served up on a bloody platter by Patriots from the South. Because of these battles, our future president received the only good news he had heard during the grimmest part of the war.

This is what Washington knew, but apparently never fully credited Appalachian soldiers for. Within a three-month and two-week period, the Overmountain Men killed Major Ferguson and slaughtered, humiliated, and forever quelled the Tories. In doing so, three months later their tactics paved the way for Cowpens, which reversed the British occupation of the South and within months forced a befuddled and naïve Redcoat general into Virginia to meet his ultimate defeat.

Why was Cornwallis so deathly afraid after these two stupendous defeats, to the point that he did not even try to go back to Charleston after his token win at Greensboro? To ultimately conquer the South, he knew that not a single Redcoat, including him, would come out alive if they chose to penetrate the Appalachian Mountains where the world's best marksmen lay in wait, coiled like a serpent.

Moreover, these mountain-bred human fighting machines obviously did not mind traveling south hundreds of miles by foot and horseback, over rugged terrain, to kill or capture every Tory and Redcoat they encountered. But more importantly, the Overmountain Men showed the new nation how to kill the other side, deflate their egos and spirit, and pile up the dead. They were not interested in any Marquess of Queensberry-type rules of engagement.

I can only assume that the producers and directors of these History Channel farces believe they hold more knowledge of the War than numerous objective military sources, including three presidents of the United States and an English general (and boss of Cornwallis) who personally felt the impact.

In this era of political (and I hope historical) correctness, I challenge the History Channel to right this bigotry and tell its audiences how the War was really won.

Football games are routinely won by big plays executed late in the game by a trailing team, and the history of our nation is no different. The southern Patriots won the day with outstanding leadership, inspiration, guts, and skills. Mountain men, by any measure, directly caused the ultimate English retreat.

With greatly naive anticipation I look forward to the new History Channel series: "How the Battles of King's Mountain and Cowpens Won the Revolutionary War."

The truth shall set them free!

CHAPTER 17
THE FRONTIER DREAMS OF FRANCOIS PIERRE DE TUBEUF

ANOTHER STRANGE SAGA came to pass in the Clinch River Valley near present day St. Paul when a French coal baron decided to leave his homeland—then embroiled in a bitter civil war—and establish a French community in the Southwest Virginia wilderness. The Frenchman, Francois Pierre De Tubeuf, did not know that he was heading toward a combat zone as the following article so eloquently reveals.

By James William Hagy *(Reprinted courtesy of the author and Virginia Magazine)*

The French Revolution of 1789 profoundly changed the lives of many men. One of these, Francois Pierre De Tubeuf, a man of noble birth, fled his native country and sought a new life on the rugged frontier of Southwest Virginia. Undoubtedly the attempt of De Tubeuf to establish a French colony in the backwoods of Virginia forms one of the strangest and saddest stories of that era. De Tubeuf lived in Normandy. When the French peasants revolted, threatening both the property and lives of the nobles, De Tubeuf communicated with Richard Smith, a London speculator who had obtained grants in Russell County amounting to about 343,000 acres through his agent in the county, Henry Smith, one of the county surveyors. Smith, like most speculators, misrepresented the land he sought to sell. A copy of what was probably the original plat has survived. With place names in French, it shows quite inaccurately a proposed city, the "Court of Justice," a road to Abingdon, and most fantastic of all, a road to Philadelphia. In 1790 De Tubeuf purchased a huge tract of the rugged, uninhabited land which was thought to total about 55,000 acres but which later proved to be much larger.

Francois Pierre De Tubeuf, artwork by Darris Stanley

After securing land in America, De Tubeuf obtained a passport on May 10, 1791, from Louis XVI, who was then still the king of France, and departed the country from Le Havre on May 30, 1791, on the ship *La Petite Nanette*. The passport issued to De Tubeuf was also valid for his sons, his niece, and five servants; however, according to Captain Pitalugo, who commanded the ship, only four servants accompanied him on the voyage to Virginia. He left France in haste and his "considerate properties" there were taken over by the National Assembly.

Upon arrival in Richmond, De Tubeuf made contact with Colonel John Harvie, who gave him a letter of introduction to Colonel Daniel Smith, a militia officer in Southwest Virginia. Not everything went well in Richmond, however, and the Frenchman began to experience difficulties that were to plague him in America. De Tubeuf and his fellow adventurers had brought with them a number of servants and tradesmen upon whom they depended, but these people were enticed away by the citizens of Richmond, who promised them a better life than they could expect on the frontier. De Tubeuf could do little to stop these defections, although he had agreements with the servants and tradesmen by which they promised four years service in return for their passage. At the end of this period, each was to receive twenty-five acres of land on which he was to pay an annual rent of two French livres.

After their Richmond adventure, De Tubeuf and his group went straight to Abingdon where Colonel Smith welcomed them and conducted them to their lands about thirty miles from Abingdon in Russell County near the little community of Castle's Woods. A number of residents of the county visited the lands the Frenchman had purchased and estimated the value to be a guinea per acre. They assured De Tubeuf that his land was of good quality and that many places were suitable for the town he planned to found on the right bank of the Clinch River. De Tubeuf had hoped to begin his settlement immediately, but Colonel Smith advised him that, in view of a number of Indian attacks which had recently occurred—one of which resulted in the murder of an entire family—this could not be done. Arrangements were then made for the Frenchmen to stay at the Russell County Courthouse, which was the nearest settlement where they would be safe.

Relations with the local people proved to be little better than with the inhabitants of Richmond. The Frenchmen had great difficulty with the English language and experienced very bad treatment at the hands of backwoodsmen every time they had to trade or bargain for goods. The "black tricks" the people played on them were very disheartening.

By the middle of October, De Tubeuf was in dire straits. He had run out of money and had not yet established his settlement. He needed protection from the Indians and a road to his land. Therefore, De Tubeuf turned to the state of Virginia for assistance. In a letter to his friend, Colonel Harvie, he outlined his great difficulties and explained that since his funds had been exhausted, he needed a loan of four hundred guineas. De Tubeuf saw himself the vanguard of a great wave of French immigrants who would begin to pour into the area the following spring. Having made plans for such an adventure before leaving France, he believed that the immigration would "enable us to make a bulwark to the frontier and put a stop to the incursions and devastations practiced by the Indians." In an appeal to Patrick Henry, he stated that assistance to him would "procure to the state of Virginia an immigration of more than twenty thousand French having at their head some of the first noblemen of France."

Of Henry he requested aid in securing six thousand Virginia pounds, and then ended his appeal with the statement, "I dare say that in obliging me you'll oblige likewise M. de le Fayette." Whether or not the facts stated in the appeal of De Tubeuf are accurate cannot be ascertained. Perhaps twenty thousand Frenchmen were anxious to settle on the frontiers of Virginia, though such a prospect seems unlikely. Up to this point, the state legislature had done but little to aid settlers on the frontier. It had not provided them with the protection they demanded; it had not built their roads; it had not made loans to them; it had shown little interest in developing the lands of Southwest Virginia. Yet the General Assembly did assist a Frenchman who had recently arrived in the Commonwealth. It appears that his appeal to the Virginians in the name of Lafayette aroused their patriotism. The marquis' name was magic, evoking memories of his aid during the Revolution and calling forth the legislature's aid on behalf of his countryman.

A bill calling for state financial assistance to De Tubeuf was introduced in the General Assembly on November 15, 1791. On December 6, Governor Henry Lee sent a letter to the house urging that the aid be granted. He concluded by appealing to the legislators to remember the blood and money that had been expended by the French in behalf of independence for the United States. On December 14, it was moved that a road should be constructed from the Russell County courthouse to the French settlement, and that six hundred pounds should be lent to the immigrants. The bill received final approval two days later. De Tubeuf was to be aided, although not in the amount he desired.

The governor then informed David Ward, an official of Russell County, that a loan had been approved for the Frenchmen and that De Tubeuf and his five friends were required to sign a bond and negotiate a mortgage as security. The amount of land to be mortgaged was left up to Ward. De Tubeuf was notified of this and on January 31, 1792, he, along with Louisa Duchesne, Charles De Spada, Cesar Lefebre, Eusebe Delaplanche, and Simon Perchet, appeared at the courthouse and executed a bond for the £600 loan.

Lacking confidence in its own money, the Virginia legislature required repayment in two thousand Spanish milled dollars or the same value in gold or silver coin by January 1, 1799. Ward took a mortgage on 15,000 acres of the best land held by the Frenchmen. Sometime during this period, De Tubeuf settled in the home of John English, high on a hill above the Clinch River. English, who had suffered two Indian attacks, the last of which resulted in the deaths of his wife and children, apparently deserted his home or gave it up to De Tubeuf with the understanding that he would be paid in the future. At least, no deed was recorded for this land. The English tract lay adjacent to that purchased by De Tubeuf.

The Frenchman had become optimistic by the fall of 1792 in spite of the fact that the "greatest part" of his associates abandoned him. The road from the courthouse had been completed at state expense, and a group of six soldiers had been stationed near his home to protect him from the Indians. The soil and climate were good, his claims were valid, and his settlement had not been molested by the Indians. He expected more immigrants to join him.

In writing to the governor and council he stated:

"Frenchmen informed of what you have done for us since our arrival here, and of the last precautions which I hope you will take, will know that they will find here another native country—that to a Frenchman, an American is a brother, a friend, and that in a free country a foreigner is not distinguished by a greater kindness and regard for him. As for me, Gentlemen, my respect and respectful attachment will last as long as my life."

The quality of the English in this letter is misleading since normally the letters to state officials were written by one of the Frenchman's sons in very broken English, and De Tubeuf himself could not write English. Despite the fact that none of the Frenchmen "could speak plain English," they seemed to get along better with their neighbors than when they first arrived. The only recorded local squabble in which De Tubeuf was involved was over a heifer which had been taken up by a neighbor in 1795.

In August 1793, De Tubeuf wrote a very cheerful letter to the governor. His youngest son had joined him and so had two other French families. In addition, many others, mainly friends and relatives, were expected to swell the ranks of his little French colony, which he began to call Sainte Marie on the Clinch. He expressed the hope that the governor would send him some of the political refugees from Cape Francais who were then in Norfolk.

After nearly two years on the frontier, De Tubeuf's plans were beginning to materialize. But the great dreams of a large French settlement suddenly ended on Election Day in April 1795. Two men, Richard Barrow and John Brown, came to the home of De Tubeuf on the pretext that they were looking for some horses. The men were invited to take a glass of wine and stay for a meal. After lingering for some time, one of the men suddenly struck the old man when his back was turned. De Tubeuf sank motionless to the floor and soon died. The two men then turned on one of his sons, Alexander. After being hit several times with a club, he was able to run from the house though badly wounded. Louise Duchesne, the niece of De Tubeuf, was also seriously injured and was thought to be dead at the time. A servant, attempting to obtain help from neighbors, was drowned crossing the Clinch River. The murderers then robbed the house taking goods valued at approximately £300.

The End of Baron De Tubeuf's Frontier Dreams, artwork by Darris Stanley

According to a newspaper account, there were twelve men involved in the conspiracy. Brown and Barrow escaped but three others, James Best, Aaron Roberts, and "the noted Obediah Paine, formerly of Bedford," were arrested as accomplices. All were sentenced in Russell County court and then taken to the district jail in Abingdon. Along with a horse thief, they escaped jail whereupon the jailer offered a reward of $20.00 each. They were quickly captured and returned to custody.

The people of the community were very anxious to bring to justice Brown and Barrow, who had escaped to the Illinois Territory. Subsequently a reward of $500.00 was offered for their arrest. The reward posters described John Brown (alias Bonds) as being about five feet eight inches tall, of about twenty-five to thirty years of age, with short black curly hair, and weighing about 180 pounds. In appearance he was said to be a sober, sedate man. Barrow, who was about the same height and weight, was said to be a slender man and was described as having "a disagreeable countenance, and down look; hath a scald head (it is said it is getting better) and always wore a handkerchief about it; he speaks thick and fast, and appears of a rattling disposition." Two men of Russell County were appointed by Governor Brooke to apprehend Brown and Barrow. In May 1796 they were caught in New Design, Illinois, but broke custody and were never brought to justice. One of those who went after them, James

McFarlane, assured the governor he would never again make such a cold journey, as the weather in those parts was "ten degrees colder than ever known before."

De Tubeuf was the motive force behind the settlement. The idea was apparently his only and the success of the venture rested on his shoulders. His death marked the beginning of the end of the French settlement. Slowly the community of Sainte Marie on the Clinch disintegrated. De Tubeuf's sons tried to carry on the work of their father, but they were too much in debt. A relative, James Campbell, who was a lawyer in Petersburg, was given power of attorney by them and they soon moved to Norfolk. Despite two acts of the legislature putting off the payment of the debt, they were unable to repay the loan which had been made to their father. They believed that the land, which was worth many times the amount of the loan, should be adequate security and that the mortgage should not be foreclosed. Finally, the two sons of De Tubeuf gave up their claims and returned to Europe in 1803. The other Frenchmen dispersed. About fifty years later the lands were sold by the state.

With the immense lands left vacant and the debt left unpaid, legal difficulties were sure to occur. Soon others began to settle on the property. Eventually accurate surveys revealed that the "French Lands," as they are still sometimes called, actually included about 150,000 acres. Because of conflicting claims and the fact that the estate lay on huge deposits of coal, it is probable that more lawsuits have been fought over the claim than over any other property in Southwest Virginia.

Thus the tragic story of Francois Pierre De Tubeuf ended. He fled from France for his life. But the New World which gave him new dreams only destroyed them. Instead of achieving success, he met death at the rough hands of Barrow and Brown. Had he lived, Southwest Virginia might today be somewhat different.

Artist's rendition of the original John English 1772 log dwelling to the left and the two-story addition to the right. The addition and brick chimneys were likely built in the 1840s by a brick maker and craftsman whose masonry style is prominently displayed in the surrounding region. Artwork by Jeff Goodson

The log dwelling was later covered with clapboard in the late 1800s. When John English first built the original one-story cabin in 1772, he was surrounded by hostile Native Americans in this, the first settler's home erected west of the Clinch River in Virginia. In fact, his wife and two sons were killed by Native Americans in 1780. After the house was burned by an arsonist on July 4, 1976, only the chimneys remained. The foremost chimney is all that remains of the house today and is the last remaining vestige of the French Settlement.

THE ABOVE LAND including the cabin site, now called Sugar Hill, was purchased by the author years after the loss of the cabin and its annexed two-story log house (circa 1840 or so). Trails and other amenities were established and opened to the public for free. Sugar Hill was recently sold to the Commonwealth of Virginia and immediately became the centerpiece of the new Clinch River State Park. Usually a new state park opens about five years after purchase, but because Sugar Hill was already a private park, the state park opened the day after recording its deed.

Note: the author recently collaborated with Amelia Townsend, a native of Big Stone Gap, Virginia, to write and produce a live-performance play about the Frenchman for production by the Shoestring Theatre Company in Oakton, Virginia. The actors are shown with the author (back row, far right).

The Frenchman's lands are described in the French-made map on the following page, which became the basis for future land and mineral claims and lawsuits for decades to come after foreclosure. More accurate surveys confirmed that the original 60,000 acre claim was vastly underestimated. One must consider that maps made at the time were based upon information provided by hunters, trappers, and a few brave surveyors who risked death by simply visiting hostile territory, much less taking the time to obtain more precise measurements and calculating exact directions.

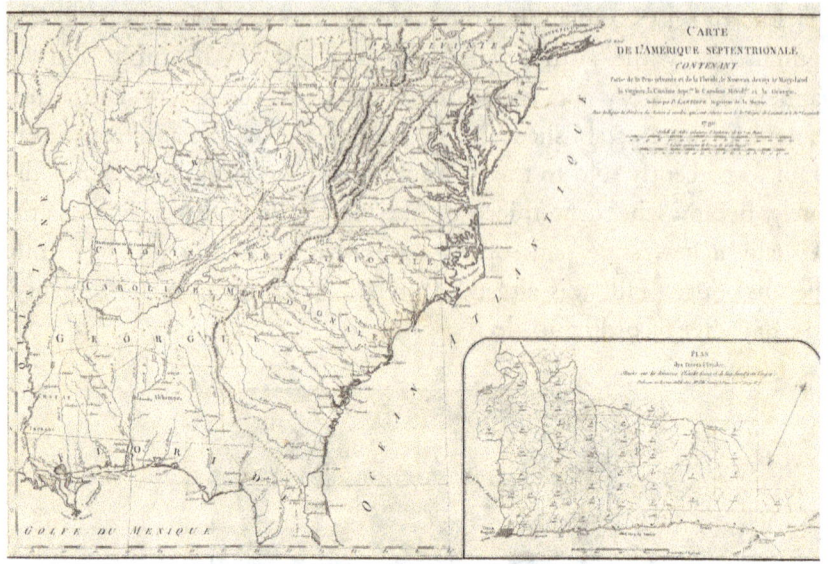

French-made maps describing the Frenchman's lands, which became the basis for future land and mineral claims and lawsuits for decades to come after foreclosure.

PART III
SOUTHWEST VIRGINIA STORIES WORTH READING

CHAPTER 18
A CIVIL WAR STORY WORTH THE TELLING OF IT: THE LONG WAY HOME

> *Author's Note: The following story tells of the harrowing days of the nation's Civil War and represents just one of thousands of accounts surrounding the strife, suffering, fear, poverty, and ruin brought on by that conflict. The story is personal to me and representative of one of the most tumultuous eras of our relatively young nation, second only to the Revolutionary War in our nation's constant evolution.*

James W. Holbrook was nineteen years old when he decided to join the Confederate Army. He and his family had just hand-hewed a yellow poplar cabin at the head of Honey Branch, a very remote community at that time situated between present day Dante and St. Paul, Virginia. He was my great-great grandfather on my Papaw Frank Kilgore's maternal side of the family.

Grandpaw Holbrook's wife, Mary Gibson Holbrook, lived to be 110 years old, and she is buried alongside her husband at Three Forks Cemetery. She outlived him by decades.

James Holbrook was not married when he went off to war and no one really knew what caused him to sign up. His family was dirt poor and had no slaves, no large farm, and no political ties. Maybe it was the adventure that youth often seek, or anger over "Yankee hordes" invading his native state or, being frugal like most Holbrooks I am kin to, he may have done it for the fifty dollar signup bonus offered by the 29th Virginia Infantry Regiment. If that is the case, he surely earned his money.

James W. Holbrook

He and his fellow green recruits mustered at Dump's Creek in Russell County in 1861, near present-day South Clinchfield. They refused to cross the Clinch River to be inducted at the Confederate headquarters in Abingdon until receiving their sign-up bonuses. Smart young men. Grandpaw Holbrook could not read or write but was able to make his initials "JWH," which may have saved his life later and prevented a great sorrow to the family he left behind.

James W. Holbrook's grave marker The inscription reads "Co. A, 29 VA INF, CSA"

The 29th is fairly well known in Virginia military circles, having fought in many wars with honor and bravery. Grandpaw's particular Company "A" fought at first in regional skirmishes, and many of the soldiers made it home periodically to help out with the crops, as was the custom at that time. Eventually though, after fighting in the Battle of the Wilderness, he ended up 300 miles from home at the Union siege of Petersburg under the division command of Major General George Pickett, a dashing southern gladiator who lost hundreds of men while charging entrenched Union forces at Cemetery Hill during the Battle of Gettysburg. Thankfully, the 29th did not fight at Gettysburg, otherwise I probably would not be writing this story.

After being routed from the breastworks of Petersburg, a segment of the Confederate troops tried to fill a gap on the outer flanks of Richmond. About 10,000 ragged Confederate soldiers, including Private J.W. Holbrook, ended up stranded at a community called Five Forks, between Petersburg and Appomattox. There the Rebel force had a decision to make. Devoid of food, shoes, ammo, and hope, and facing Union forces that stood at 22,000 well-supplied soldiers, the options were to die or surrender. The commanding officer knew the end of the war was near and elected to save himself and his exhausted loyal soldiers.

Breastworks at Petersburg

Confederate dead, Petersburg

To call the ensuing April 1, 1865, fight with the Yankees a "battle" is a little bit of a stretch compared to the 29th's bout at Cold Harbor and other bloodlettings so frequent in the world's first highly mechanized war. Several Union soldiers had repeating "high tech" rifles during the Five Forks rout (as they also did during Gettysburg), and the Confederates had zero. This mix of outdated tactics pitted against mass-killing techniques became America's most costly war in people lost and countryside devastated.

Battle Flag captured, artwork by Darris Stanley

Many of the starving Confederates at Five Forks were gathered up and freighted on Yankee ships to Hart's Island off the banks of New York City. Grandpaw and 2,400 of his buddies, either by luck or chance, were incarcerated in that dark, dank, dingy, isolated prison on April 7th, only two days before the war ended at Appomattox on April 9, 1865. At Hart's Island they joined other longer-term prisoners of war. Hauling Rebel prisoners back to their home states was not on the Union's priority list at that time, so four months went by before they loaded up all 3,413 rebel POWs (minus 235 who died from exposure and disease) onto freight ships once again and ferried them back to the Virginia coast and beyond.

Photo of Confederate POWs, Five Forks (of course I wonder
if my Grandpaw Holbrook is pictured amongst them)

There were no bands playing, Confederate flags waving, or soup kitchens waiting. It was work or starve, with nothing to their names except the meager shoes and clothes the prison warden had to offer. Many of the Confederate POWs lived within a few days' walk from the coast. Others were much farther away from home. Grandpaw Holbrook may have walked and hitched an occasional train ride the farthest of his Virginia comrades. It had to seem that way to him as he put one foot in front of the other, seeking work for food few Virginians had to spare and water that was fit to drink.

The farther he traveled westward toward Honey Branch, the more he ran into Union sympathizers who were not all that grateful toward the Confederate cause. Some of these Union loyalists were such from the beginning of the war, while others converted when the Confederacy started requisitioning (stealing) food from soldiers' families to keep the fight going. Several Confederates converted to the Union side, but many of them stuck to their oath until forced to take the Union pledge or go without pensions.

The History and Culture of Coalfields Southwest Virginia

The Honey Branch log cabin James W. Holbrook helped build near St. Paul, Virginia. The author and his family lived here in the 1950s, the last descendants of J.W. to do so. Photo by Don Askins, 1978

Several months after the war ended, Grandpaw Holbrook crossed the Clinch River at Wheeler's Ford. His way home was just a mile up Lick Creek, then a hard left up a lonely horse trail a few more miles along his beloved Honey Branch Creek (then called the Left Fork of Lick Creek).

Meanwhile, Grandpaw's family had not heard of or from him in five years, so they realistically gave him up for dead. Their fresh-faced, doe-eyed, slender boy was gone, and they had to work around the clock to eke out a meager subsistence-farm living for his surviving siblings, all the while being wary of bushwhackers, scalawags, and night riders who caused much grief during and after the war.

So it was when Grandpaw Holbrook finally spied the small, two-story poplar log cabin straight up the hollow, his heart beating with anticipation, his belly ready for Momma's squirrel gravy and biscuits, with visions of hugging his big family all in one big swoop dancing in his head. His bent-over parents were tending the large garden when one of their younger sons, who was catching crawdads in the creek, spotted a bearded, scruffy, gaunt figure of a man. Running at top speed, the little boy reported that this unknown sojourner was surely looking for plunder, or worse.

Expecting a son's welcome, if not that of a conquering hero, Grandpaw Holbrook was surely surprised when his father cocked a rusted pistol in his face. "Stay where you are and state your business," he recalled being told.

"I'm James, your son! For God's sake don't shoot me after all I've been through!"

"You are a liar, James is dead," was his father's reply.

"I ain't dead as can plainly be seen!" was his shaky reply. Then it dawned on him that after numerous battles and prison, his resulting tattered clothes, sunken eyes, and skeletal frame were nothing like his photo the family had commissioned before he headed to Dump's Creek.

Then Grandpaw Holbrook started rattling off names of his kin, deceased and some he hoped were still alive. "That don't mean nothing," his father continued, "anyone can read them off our graveyard down the holler. You come right by it!"

James Holbrook's homecoming, artwork by Darris Stanley

By this time his mother came to join the interrogation, not fearing much danger since the ragged scarecrow of a man was unarmed and barely able to stand. "You say you are my son do ye?" she asked with great skepticism.

"Yes, Mother, it's me!" he cried.

"Well, you helped build this cabin before you took off to war after me pleading with you not to go. Tell me where you slept and what is on the inside wall that you put there," she queried.

James hesitated. He knew he'd slept in the loft facing the north end of the house, but he didn't know if she was referring to a picture, a gun, a tool, or a string of dried beans, and he was afraid to muff too many more questions. Then it dawned on him. "On the second log up from the floor you showed me how to carve my initials, JWH, the only letters I ever learned."

The ensuing shouts, crying, and swooping embraces had to be spine-chilling.

My Papaw Frank Kilgore remembered his Grandpaw James Holbrook very well. Papaw Kilgore was born in 1895 and Grandpaw Holbrook died in 1923, so there were many years of them working together and playing checkers when the chores were done or the snow and bitter winds swept the little cabin. Vast amounts of firewood had to be cut each year to keep the drafty cabin bearable, and Papaw Kilgore, from age six until he went to work in the coal mines at age fifteen, helped all he could.

Sabra Ann Holbrook Kilgore visiting the ancestral Kilgore Fort House on Moccasin Creek in Scott County in the 1930s. Her father was James Holbrook. His long trek back from a federal POW prison near New York City was the basis for his family's generational negative opinion of all things New York. Thankfully we got over it 140 years later.

One dreary winter day, while playing checkers with Grandpaw Holbrook, Pawpaw Kilgore recalled being happy to be playing a game instead of hand-sawing, chopping, and hauling wood in sloppy weather. Just as the game commenced, Grandpaw Holbrook sprung to his feet, knocked over the checkerboard, checkers and all, and stuck his hickory cane through the windowpane facing toward the narrow dirt road. "Let them sneak up on us why don't you boy!" he screamed. This ruckus caused Grandmaw Holbrook to come scurrying in to see what all the commotion was about.

"James! Set down and quit scaring the boy! You done broke out part of the winder; stick your handkerchief in it before we freeze to death!" Then she walked out.

A very confused grandson watched as his Grandpaw looked around the room and then spied the checkerboard and scattered checkers along the rough puncheon floor. "What did you do that for boy?" he asked, incredulously.

Papaw Kilgore had never heard of post-traumatic stress disorder or dementia, but he knew something wasn't right. They finished the checkers game and went to bed.

John Holbrook and Nancy Jordan Holbrook, parents of James W. Holbrook and his eleven siblings

Mary Elizabeth (Gibson) Holbrook, widow of James Holbrook, sitting with her sister sometime in the 1940s, smoking her clay pipe in the same cabin her late husband helped build prior to going to war

Sabra Holbrook at her loom, 1950s

111-Year-Old Woman Smokes Now, But Not When Younger

By HAMPTON OSBORNE
Special Correspondent

Clintwood, Va. — (Spl) — It looked good to see her smoking her old, long stem pipe; it reminded me of my grandmother who smoked one just like the one she was using.

I asked her of women who smoked in old age ever smoked when they were young. Aunt Mary Elizabeth Holbrook, age 111, didn't answer for a minute. Her shocked reply was, "Why—no, we wouldn't have thought of such a thing. We smoke after we become old to stimulate us a bit."

Mrs. Holbrook said she smokes only after meals and before retiring at night.

Probably the oldest living person in Dickenson County, she also has another use for tobacco, it was revealed, when she insisted on showing her burial clothing. A beautiful black cashmere dress unlike anything on the market today both in quality and tailoring was carefully put away. With it a handsome silk scarf was wrapped around a large twist of tobacco, all put a-way 35 years ago, after her husband bought her burial dress long before his death.

Why the tobacco was in the scarf Aunt Mary Elizabeth explained, "That keeps the old bugs from ruining it. Tobacco was used long before moth balls came into use to keep moths from destroying clothes."

Mary E. Holbrook ... Over a Century

A most likeable old lady and alert beyond one's expectations, considering her age, Mrs. Holbrook can recall many incidents of her early childhood as though they were but yesterday.

The terrible depredations of the Civil War and the atrocities committed by the Bushwhackers who made life miserable among peaceful folk living in rural Dickenson and Russell Counties are remembered with very little respect by Aunt Mary. "They were as low-down and mean as could be," she said in a manner that left little doubt that she was right about it.

Near the town of Dante, a camp of Negroes remained sometime, but she couldn't remember whether they were kept in custody by Rebels or Yankees.

Her Husband's Picture

Her husband, J. W. Holbrook, saw service in the most noted battles of the war, including the famous Battle of the Wilderness. His picture, enlarged in a wide, wooden frame in style many years ago, was on the wall. Holbrook was wearing his uniform. Her husband was captured and taken prisoner on Hart's Island, where he remained a year after the war ended, during which time Aunt Mary almost gave him up for dead.

She told of cooking on the fireplace in which the Dutch oven and the old iron kettle were about the only cooking vessels of that day. She told of baking ash cakes in which the cornmeal dough was wrapped in a clean cloth or husk of corn and put in the ashes under the fore stick of a wood fire.

She still has the candle mold from which she made candles for her family when she was a small girl.

Her children are: Sabra, married to Hugh Kilgore, Caroline married to Andrew Minton, Mary, married to Clinton Robinson; Malissia, married to Milton French, with whom Mrs. Holbrook lives; Henry Holbrook and Nelson Holbrook, who died at the age of four months.

She said that she had had a "Hope" for the past fifty years; meaning that she had been a Christian for that length of time.

Now very childish and easily offended, as are all old people, she cried when I prepared to leave and seemed not to understand why I could not stay a longer time.

Memories of her school days she recalled with a degree of accuracy and detail. She attended school in a small log building in which the good earth served as a floor. A large wide fireplace provided the heat for the room. Seats were long logs split and hewed flat with a broad ax.

She could not remember the kind of school books used in her day. She told of her first day in school. Her teacher was Whetzel Wampler, who like all teachers of his day was a firm believer in law and order in the school room. She was afraid of him, so when he called class in order to teach her the ABC's, she began to cry and would not come up to recite. An older girl asked Schoolmaster Wampler to allow her to have her lessons in her seat. Wampler agreed, and this plan was carried out throughout the school term.

She remembered some of the ministers of her early childhood. She attended church where Elder Morgan Lipps, a noted Baptist minister in pioneer days preached in Wise, Russell and Dickenson Counties. Lipps served this section as member in the General Assembly for some time.

She recalled hearing Rev. Alfred Holbrook and Rev. Jerry Wampler, who were noted Methodists in this section of the great Southwest.

She was skillful in the weaving of yarn and linen cloth and says that she made most of her children's clothing, using such combination of coloring as "hickory bark and alum" to give a proper variety. She kept sheep and did the whole process of manufacturing from the wool to the finished product

As a proof of her skill she had a bedspread brought from her trunk which she had made some 80 years ago. It was of faultless design and workmanship, looked almost to be new. She made one for each of her children.

She still has her old side saddle which was in vogue in her early life. It had a velvet top and was about 50 years old.

Newspaper article about Mary Elizabeth Holbrook, widow of James W. Holbrook, when she was 111 years old. The newspaper account of her age conflicts with the government data on her tombstone. She was only 110.

Mary Elizabeth Holbrook's tombstone

CHAPTER 19
SPECIAL FEATURE: TWO MOUNTAIN BOYS GO TO WAR

In recognition of the thousands of Appalachian veterans of the Army, Navy, Air Force, Marines, and Coast Guard who have served our country.

ONLY AS WE age and hone the art of looking at the world through the eyes of others do we have true insight. Such is the case for those of us who have not lived the terrible experience of war except through stories, movies, old photos, veterans, and graveyards.

A decade-ago visit to the serene Holbook family cemetery brought into focus how improbable it must have seemed to our World War II generation of Appalachian young men just how drastically their lives would change. How could they have known that a life of cutting trees with axes and cross-cut saws; grubbing stumps with picks and mattocks; clearing stones by hand and horse sled from steep mountain farms; mining coal with hand-turned breast augers, picks, and shovels; digging roots and herbs to sell for pennies; staying up all moonlit night to keep the moonshine still fired up and guarded from "revenoors"; brawling in the nearest town on Saturday nights; and going to dances to give the prettiest girls the "brush off" wouldn't last? That the lives of these starlet boys could transition seemingly overnight to basic training with other young men from every state in the nation, then finding themselves far away from their mountain redoubts in war-torn Europe or the jungle killing fields of the Pacific Theatre.

W.N. Holbrook and Arthur Kilgore

Arthur Kilgore, my father, and his best friend and cousin, W. N. Holbrook quit school at very young ages and entertained themselves with learning every tree and animal in the woods and becoming experts at shooting squirrels in the head with .22 rifles and stopping lightning-fast grouse on the fly with a single-shot Winchester 20-gauge shotgun. Stealth, young reflexes, and the family's need for meat on the table forged hunters and future warriors throughout the Appalachian Mountains. Drill sergeants and war planners in every branch of the military sought out mountain boys because of their shooting skills, self-discipline, patriotism, respect for authority, and a fierce loyalty to their flag and buddies. In short, these rangy mountain boys made superb fighters and have produced hero after hero in our country's military history.

W. N. Holbrook was the first to go to war. After an expedited training period, he ultimately found himself assigned to the 91st Engineers, a unit that saw much action throughout Europe and later found themselves in the midst of the Battle of the Bulge. W. N. was killed on December 21, 1944, in a battle Allied military experts denied could happen despite numerous scouting reports that the Germans were preparing a "do-or-die" counter-attack in the forests of Belgium. He and 19,000 other soldiers returned home in military coffins; 60,000 more were maimed or wounded.

W.N. 's family and friends carried his remains up the steep hill above his beloved home on Honey Branch near St. Paul, Virginia. Hemlocks were planted by his father, Alfred, in the gap of the ridge, and W. N. laid there, a military grave marker resting at his head, while he patiently waited to be joined by his parents and many of his fourteen siblings as they passed away from mostly natural causes.

The Holbrook Cemetery sits through the seasons, the hemlock trees continuing to grow and shade out all understory. The small American flag planted near W. N.'s military headstone constantly waves in the prevailing breeze that funnels through the small gap. Flag after wind-tattered flag is replaced by surviving family members as dignity dictates.

After W.N.'s funeral, it was time for my dad to accept the U.S. Army's invitation for an all-expense-paid trip to Europe, along with a chance to show off the marksmanship skills honed in the hollers and ridges of one the nation's most remote and hardy subcultures, the Central Appalachians.

Arthur Kilgore

Dad won his division's shooting competition, and the top ten sharpshooters (mostly from the mountains, the deep South, farms and ranches) were given a weekend pass just before shipping out to war.

They made fun of their New Jersey buddies who shot into the ground far more frequently than nailing distant targets. Once in Europe, these mountain ninjas found themselves at risk while their less-accurate companions were relegated to the relative safety of providing food, ordnance, and supplies to the human spear tips that clashed with well-trained but retreating German forces.

Fortunately for dad, the war in Europe was in its last throes when he arrived, and his unit, the 104th Infantry Division ("Timberwolves"), had a need for mop-up units to chase down the last of the hardened SS troops who used their own countrymen, mostly young boys and old men, as diversionary shields as they retreated and attempted to blend in with civilians. The 104th had seen heavy action in Northern France, the Rhineland, and Central Europe, so bringing down the SS stragglers was more akin to hunting weasels in the hills than full-scale combat.

One of the three military memorials located in St. Paul, a town of 1,000 citizens

Once the war with Germany ended, thousands of American troops were hurriedly sent to the West Coast and positioned to proceed by flotillas to Japan for the invasion of the Imperial homeland. U.S. losses were projected to be nearly a million casualties. A half-million Purple Hearts were ordered in advance of what was called "Operation Downfall." The carnage to Japan's military and civilian populations was projected to be many times more than American losses.

By this time, most of Japan's air defenses had been disabled, and waves of American bombers leveled and burned great swaths of Tokyo and other population and manufacturing centers. In one night raid of the nation's capitol, the city endured 100,000 fiery deaths from relatively new napalm bombs. Hundreds of thousands of Japanese soldiers and civilians died horrendous deaths during these ceaseless air raids, yet Japan's leaders vowed to fight until the last breath.

Many post-war critics typed away from the safety of their office desks about how President Truman's bombing of Hiroshima and Nagasaki was overly brutal and unnecessary. They apparently were not among the hundreds of thousands of American soldiers fresh from Europe or expedited basic training being loaded onto hundreds of ships for what could have become a loss of American lives that would eclipse fatalities sustained during the entire Civil War.

My dad, who was poised to load onto one of those ships bound for Japan, found many reasons to shout at the TV during his later years, but his most vocal diatribes were aimed at any "soft-bellied" critics of President Truman. As for Japanese fatalities, two atomic bombs actually saved millions of that country's people who would have died if a conventional war had ensued. This morbid calculation lesson is very difficult to even imagine, much less understand the President's agony.

Fresh from college back in the 1970s, I tried to impress my dad with an objective analysis of how our war veterans ultimately fought for and secured the right of any and all Americans to assemble and peacefully protest the war of his or her choice. Thankfully I did not talk about flag burnings. That pseudo-intellectual effort was a big mistake on my part.

When I visited the Holbrook Cemetery in the gap of the ridge right after the great snowstorm of 2009, I reflected upon my now-deceased father and his unfaltering loyalty to our nation. I stared at the cold, somber military gravestone of his best friend for several spine-tingling minutes as the frigid wind whispered through the hemlocks. Only then did I fully appreciate the vast difference between theory and reality.

The History and Culture of Coalfields Southwest Virginia

W.N. Holbrook's gravesite during the great snowstorm of 2009

CHAPTER 20
GIVING PRESIDENT JIMMY CARTER A JAR OF HONEY FROM HONEY BRANCH

I was born and raised in a "holler" (hollow) named Honey Branch. It is a five-mile-long, very narrow suburb of maybe 200 residents between St. Paul and Dante, Virginia. In the 1950s and 1960s, a World War II veteran resided in nearly every household there and elsewhere in Appalachia. These vets likely worked in a coal mine, a tipple, or a prep plant, drove a coal truck, worked for the railroad, or logged. They were tough, tough, men and did not brook much nonsense. Our cousin, Virginia Kilgore, was only one of two women in the whole county of Wise to join the Women's Army Corps (WACS). We were very proud of her as well.

ONE WARTIME DESERTER lived at the head of the holler and no one respected him. Except, occasionally, he and my dad (also a vet, honorably discharged) would make moonshine whiskey together.

Allen deserted the U.S. Army after his brother was killed at the Battle of the Bulge and just prior to being shipped out to Europe himself. He lived in the woods above his parents' house in a lean-to during the warm months, and in an old "dog hole" abandoned coal mine in the winter. Therein he enjoyed 54-degree temperatures, plenty of water, and total darkness.

His mom would place food out on her back porch every day or so, and he would slip down at night and take it back to his hideouts. After the war was over, he got careless and started staying in the relatively cozy family home a night or two a week.

The military police knew how to catch most deserters that were "scouting," a term sometimes used for AWOLS that hid out in the big cities, thick woods, bayous, and deserts throughout America. After a couple of months passed by, the M.P.s would simply watch "Momma's house." Sooner or later the frightened absconder would make a mistake.

Allen was thus captured and dishonorably discharged after doing time in the brig and watching his uniform burn in front of fellow soldiers. He never held a real job, rarely took a bath, and was pretty nasty in speech and habit all around. The other vets I knew were proud, supported their families, voted in every election, and kept the same job until they retired. "Solid as a rock" described them to a tee.

The name Honey Branch inspired me later in life in a situation I could not have imagined while growing up in a hardscrabble world. My dad raised honeybees and started his first hive from a swarm that flew around me as I was wading up the creek, looking for muskrats to trap. The swarm, I thought, was trying to land on me, so I lay down in the creek until they settled around the queen in a big willow tree branch overhead. Dad caught them and started his own honeybee colony. As the loyal bees repeatedly exiled the next new queen and swarmed, he added more bee boxes until we had a dozen or so in a big bee village on the steep hillside overlooking our small, drafty, frame house. We had fresh honey and comb to spare.

Years later, while attending Clinch Valley College (now known as the The University of Virginia's College at Wise, or UVAW) I met a sociology professor named Helen Lewis. I signed up for an Appalachian Seminar night class she taught while I was working full time and starting a family. I took college very seriously, unlike my high school attitude. Later on, my professors were impressed that I worked full-time while attending college full-time. It never occurred to me that I had a choice.

Dr. Lewis suggested that, as a class project, I start a citizens' group of local people to push for better strip-mining reclamation laws. At that time, Virginia was dead last in the nation when it came to regulating this very earth-shattering coal mining method. Little did she know that I would take my mission to heart so zealously, nor did either of us fathom that my activities would later end her job.

Years later, as she was delivering somewhat of a returned-exile homecoming speech at the college, I learned for the first time that the dozen or so students prior to me she had suggested take on this project never did a thing; apparently I thought it was an honor to have a "doctor" express confidence in me. She recently passed on at the age of 97. She is known in the mountain academic world as the grandmother of Appalachian Studies. In 1974, she and I creatively put together the first program of its kind to my knowledge. I graduated with honors and had no clue what that meant as I didn't hang around the campus when the day was done. One of my professors spent ten dollars for me to rent a gown and cap as the graduation started since I had a tight budget.

The problem with unfettered strip mining was real. Coal companies could mine within five feet of their neighbors' property lines. They sometimes blasted rocks through the roofs of buildings, including the gymnasium and covered pool at our college. Dynamite and ammonium nitrate-powered explosions cracked house foundations, and one mega-blast registered on the Richter Scale over 120 miles away at Virginia Tech. One company rolled a Volkswagen-sized rock onto the Norton Elementary School playground. Several private cemeteries were disturbed, and mining near secondary public roads caused landslides and collapsed shoulders while overloaded coal trucks busted pavement and spilled coal dust onto the roads by the tons. Creeks were filled with uprooted trees, rocks, dirt, and silt to the point that local flooding was frequent and aquatic life rare.

A fiery opponent (referred to later in this story) of federal "meddling" owned a coal company that many years after the federal law and regulations were enacted ignored inspectors as much as he could. This particular law forbade nighttime excavation above occupied dwellings. A huge rock was thusly rolled down the steep hill below and killed a baby who was sleeping in his crib. This disaster made national news but no criminal charges against the machine operator or the company were filed. And all this mayhem was just in my little part of coalfield Appalachia, yet this hate of the federal law was not so rare in the coalfields.

It was as if free-range Hell's Angels had been provided bulldozers, augers, drills, and dynamite instead of Harleys.

Local resistance toward proposed federal mining restrictions was fierce in many powerful circles as I took my slideshow (now called PowerPoint) on the road. The color photos depicted muddy streams, huge landslides, blasted homes, and soaring highwalls to the dozens of civic groups, schools, and public hearings that allowed me in. Things sometimes got tense.

I was often the only person in a packed room or auditorium openly and loudly supporting the proposed federal surface-mining act. I was routinely threatened but decided not to back down.

An advocacy group I founded in 1975, the Virginia Citizens for Better Reclamation (VCBR), became nationally known because of our coalfield roots and persistence. Our membership was mostly made up of United Mine Workers underground miners, blasting victims, the occasional homegrown conservationist, and a few "outsiders" that came to appreciate our mountains. Back then, we natives mostly took our ancient, biologically diverse hills for granted.

VCBR was also known, and begrudgingly respected at times, for not advocating the abolition of strip mining. This position caused many national environmental groups to shun or verbally attack us (once in a D.C. church). In other words, we equally enraged both extreme sides of the issue.

This experience taught me that only lazy or stupid people pursue an "all-or-nothing" position on important issues. Getting nothing is not too smart, and those that get it usually quit trying to do anything positive.

The federal law had already passed Congress once, but President Gerald Ford vetoed it and a vote to override him fell short. Then Jimmy Carter took office and promised to sign the bill if it got to his desk. We went to work even harder.

After kicking off the initial congressional hearings with my slideshow before the House Natural Resource Committee chaired by

Congressman Morris Udall, I was very pleased to see that progress was being made. As I walked down the steps of the Capitol, after completely debunking the industry's fake reclamation presentations, a coal operator (and "high-powered" lawyer) and two of his friends confronted me with not-so-subtle predictions of my safety back home.

My aggressive reaction apparently was not what they anticipated. The lawyer was upset that Congress had just viewed authentic photos of strip-mining abuse instead of the doctored photos circulated by him and the mining lobbyists that showed happy cattle dining on thickly grassed strip mines. That particular photographed site they handed out was two miles from my small, rented house. The "pasture" did not have a fence around it. The cattle had been unloaded from a livestock trailer and the serene pictures taken, then the bovines were loaded back up. That exposé, plus my un-doctored pictures of holes in the roofs of houses, the damaged college gymnasium and swimming pool, 300 to 400-foot-long landslides, mud-laden creeks, and spilled coal covering public roads were potent. Again I refused to back down; it's just not in our mountain culture to run from bullies.

After the aforesaid sidewalk confrontation, I soon found myself back in Washington, D.C., appearing before the U.S. Senate as the federal strip mining bill kept moving forward. I later accompanied members of the House and Senate on a helicopter tour above the strip mines of Southwest Virginia. They were speechless at what they saw.

During the flyover, I sat next to Chairman Udall as we approached a strip mining site near the Wise Airport where dozens of landslides extended hundreds of feet down slope before slamming into streams. The coal operator, Jerry, was there to explain this undeniable carnage by stating that his company was new at strip mining and they didn't realize what would happen.

I cut him off abruptly and asked him if he was aware of the laws of physics, particularly gravity. He turned very red-faced. Then I pointed out that his father started the first strip mine in Wise County in 1948. I then wondered very out loud just how was it that by the 1960s and 70s they had not learned these laws of physics since surely there were no state laws to learn, etc..

I was on a roll, assuming that my personal safety was assured by the U.S. Government.

Chairman Udall called us down and got on the helicopter to leave. When I started to climb on board he said, for the first time, that he and his entourage were flying directly to West Virginia next. He suggested that I could catch a ride with one of "those gentlemen," one being the coal operator I had just fricasseed on his own property, and the other a state mining inspector who just heard me call his agency a coal industry lap dog.

After climbing up a collapsed highwall to avoid having to ask anyone for a favor, especially a hostile one, I started walking east toward my home, a mere twenty miles away.

The state inspector waited until Jerry left as I topped the ridge above the high wall before shouting at me, "Get your sorry butt down here!"

I sheepishly climbed into the state Jeep with the inspector, who laughed at my predicament but finally conceded that his agency had its hands tied due to the coal industry's political might in Richmond. He basically agreed to my lap dog theory and later became a top-notch federal strip mine inspector.

What I didn't realize during the drama was that the *Washington Post* photographer accompanying us had climbed the highwall after me and photographed the helicopter sitting on the strip mine bench with a background of landslides and waste as far as the camera could capture. I was in the forefront of the photo, looking lean, determined, and unhappy.

The photo and Sunday article about the federal act made it onto the front page above the crease, further cementing among the coal industry that I was solely to blame for slowing down their ransacking of coalfield Appalachia. Obviously I was not the sole reason the bill passed. But back home I was the native son who saw things much differently than the industry-dominated political and social circles that prospered the most from "shoot and shove" strip mining.

Environmentalist Frank Kilgore examines area of a worked-out Wise County, Virginia, strip mine. Helicopter carries agent of the Virginia Division of Mine Land Reclamation. (PHOTO CREDIT: Washington Post photo by Ken Feil, Illustrates story slugged COAL, by Paul G. Edwards (Post), to move Monday)

Va. Strip Mining Brings Prosperity, Woes

by Paul G. Edwards

July 31, 1977

(reprinted and truncated with permission)

From a helicopter fluttering through the hot haze over Virginia's Cumberland Mountains 325 miles southwest of Washington, the passenger can watch the good and bad effects of the region's coal boom real past below.

In the streets of Wise and Norton towns that declined for 25 years during the regional recession that made Appalachia synonymous with hard times, coal trucks and late model automobiles pass in a steady stream. New housing dots the hillsides around the towns and the main roads are lined with the low, steel structures that house the office of surface mine operators and heavy equipment dealers.

The banks that once occupied the ground floors of aging red brick buildings in town centers now stand out as scattered, new structures on the edge of black parking lots.

Everywhere, the shiny outlets of the fast food chains suggest a rising personal disposable income in an area where family nutrition long relied on food stamps and garden plots.

These are the signs of prosperity, but even a brief helicopter flight also shows that this prosperity arrived at a cost.

Northwest of Wise, the steep slopes of Little Black Mountain lie bare, stripped of the hardwood forests that slopes are covered with the rocky rubble that was ripped away to reach the thin seams of coal that run through the mountain.

On the edge of Norton, the still raw site of a complete hilltop mine reaches to within a few feet of the back doors of the modest home on 13th Street.

One of the 13th Street residents, retired coal miner, Ewin Davison, 65, said in an interview that the dust created by the months-long strip mining operation covered the neighborhood so thickly that his 14-year-old son, Jeffrey Lynn, contracted silicosis.

Davidson also said blasting at the mine site broke windows and cracked the chimney of his home and sent rocks flying through the roofs of at least two houses in the area.

About two blocks away on Park Avenue, Norton's main streets, Mrs. Joseph Fischer showed visitors what she said was damage caused to her 12-year-old brick home by strip mine blasting. It included a four-foot crack in the block walls of the basement and wide separations between the basement floor and walls.

Most of the strip mines, of course, are located in lightly populated rural areas, but the mines also have caused complaints. In small communities of Lee County near Pennington Gap, residents contend that recent flooding of their low-lying homes was caused by rapid runoff from stripped areas high on the mountainsides.

Mud covered roads in front of the homes and buried tomato plants and other vegetables in their garden, they said, as the heavy rains of late spring carried slit away from the mine sites.

Against this background of prosperity and grievances - both stimulated by strip mining - some dramatic developments are occurring in Virginia's coal-fields.

For the first time, a citizens organization of coal field residents - the still small but rapidly growing Virginia Citizens for Better Reclamation (VCBR) - is increasing pressure for local, state and federal government controls on mining.

At the same time, the state agency that regulates strip mining is about to impose significantly more stringent regulations on mining methods and Congress is near enactment of even tougher federal strip mine restraints.

There continues to be fierce debates over how effective these proposed regulations will be in limiting the adverse effects of strip mining. There also are questions about how much they will add to the price of coal, a major factor in rising electric bills.

In Virginia, these debates are developing what appear to the last years of the controversial strip mining industry. According to figures recently published by the state planning district commissions in the coal fields, strip mine production in Virginia should total 12.4 million tons this year, about one-third of the state's total coal production.

It is projected to decline steadily until 1990 when Virginia's surface mine reserves are expected to be depleted. By then, all of Virginia's coal will come from deep mines, from which production is projected to rise from about 26 million tons this year to 60 million tons by 1990.

But before the strip mining era ends in Virginia, the planning commissions' surveys predict that about 127 square miles in seven counties will have been disturbed. This would be roughly 8 per cent of the region in which the mines are located. The majority of this area, about 75 square miles, already was mined by 1975, the surveys showed.

There appear to be three explanations for the pressure for tougher strip mine regulations so late in the day of strip mining in Virginia. One is that mining activity increased rapidly after the 1973 Arab Oil embargo and attracted more complaints. Another is that Virginia strip mining is occurring at a time of proposed federal regulation of a growing nationwide industry.

The third reason appears to be Frank Kilgore, a 25-year-old descendant of 18th century Irish settlers of Southwest Virginia and the founder of VCBR. Kilgore, the son and grandson of coal miners, lives with his wife and two children in Honey Branch hollow near the town of St. Paul on the eastern edge of Virginia's coal fields.

He understands as well as anyone why it has taken so long for anyone to start a movement for improved strip mine reclamation practices in Southwest Virginia, a part of the country that tends to resist advice from "outsiders."

"People just don't have the effectiveness in getting the government to act in this area that they do in other places," he said in an interview. "Looking down here - rocks through the roofs of houses and silicosis from the dust created by strip mining."

Kilgore said he has wanted to work for strip mine controls ever since he was about 12 years old and first saw the results of strip mining on hunting trips with his father near Honey Branch.

He organized VCBR and put together a slideshow used to promote the organization in 1976 on a Southern Appalachian leadership grant. The organization, he said, has been financed during the first 18 months of its activities on grants totaling $18,000 from the Ford Foundation and churches.

Kilgore said he has been the target of threats and assaults since he began his campaign for strip mine controls. He said someone in a passing car fired a shot at him last Christmas Eve as he stood in the yard of his home. The driver of what appeared to him to be the same car also tried to force him off a mountainous road one night as he drove home from nearby Wise.

Nevertheless, Kilgore said VCBR has steadily grown to 350 members and is gaining influence partly because it is based in the coal fields and includes coal miners.

"At least people are talking in the open about better reclamation of mined land." he said. "That has never happened down here before."

Kilgore says the organization does not oppose strip mining - "That would be ridiculous in the coal fields" - but advocates regulations that would prevent pushing spoil (land stripped from above the coal seam) down the mountainsides and reduce erosion that fills coal field streams with silt.

VCBR also is working for tighter regulation of blasting that would prevent the kind of damage reported by Norton residents. Kilgore said that Edward S. Grandis, VCBR's only full time employee, has drafted major provisions restricting blasting that is contained in the federal legislation.

"I hate to see the federal government take over strip mining regulation" Kilgore said, "but the state has taken a hands-off policy. The basic provisions in the federal bill couldn't be passed in Virginia in 20 years."

Surface mine operators have strongly opposed the federal bill. Some of them have claimed that a provision requiring operators to restore stripped land to its original contour would end s

\trip mining in Virginia because of the steep slopes in its coal fields.

However, James A. Brown Jr., one of the most successful coal operators in Wise County, believes that stripping will continue under the federal bill-but at a higher price to consumers and with higher profits for operators.

[end of article]

Author's Note: The rest of this story should be too embarrassing to tell, but how does one write an entire book of history and culture without admitting to some awful, and maybe funny, missteps? Here I go:

I received a call a few days before the law (formally the Surface Mining Control and Reclamation Act of 1977, "SMCRA") was to be signed by President Jimmy Carter in the White House Rose Garden. I had made friends with one moderate national environmental group, and the director had gotten me an invitation to attend. I was excited but nearly penniless. Every cent I earned was spoken for. I grossed about $130 per week. So VCBR's membership passed the hat and raised enough gas money to see me off to the nation's capitol, where I "stayed all night" with my hostess and her husband.

The next day we entered the White House unsearched. In those days security was lax, and the strapping Secret Service agents were friendly and welcoming. That was about to change.

My first disappointment was that the plan for me to stand near the President as he signed this landmark legislation was changed at the last minute. I was the only coalfield resident at the event, my hostess informed me, so Congressman Udall wanted me front and center.

As we were being lined up by the White House photographer, he evidently noticed my green tee shirt and blue jeans. Not having any "dress-up" clothes, I figured that Jimmy, a peanut farmer after all, would not mind. The photographer felt differently.

He stuck me in the third row, where my shirt and pants would not spoil his otherwise perfect photo of 1970s suits and dresses worn by what I assumed were very rich people. Only my bushy hair, high cheekbone, and one beady brown eye were visible in the photo. But that slight turned out to be a relatively minor setback.

Signing ceremony for the Surface Mining Control and Reclamation Act of 1977, "SMCRA"

Although it was August and very hot, I had a light jacket draped over my arm. Under it was a quart of my dad's honey and on a piece of masking tape in all caps I had hand-written: "HONEY FROM

HONEY BRANCH, VIRGINIA FOR JIMMY CARTER (and his family)."

I was amazed at how clever this would be, and envisioned that when I went through the line to shake the President's hand I would whip out the jar of honey and present it to him. Of course he would then read the label out loud. Then the next morning, the President of the United States of America would sit at the White House kitchen table and share the sweet contents with Rosalynn and Amy over hot buttered "cathead" biscuits. I was set.

Everything was going great while I was shaking the President's hand as Chairman Udall bent down to tell him about my role in supporting the Act. Then I pulled out my gift and "reached" the honey jar toward the President. The now *un*-friendly Secret Service agents jumped forward to grab this gift of appreciation, but I was too quick.

I recoiled and backed several feet onto the Rose Garden portico and would not let go of the treasure. When one of the agents grabbed my forearm, I "bowed up," a common defensive (and offensive) measure well-meaning rednecks often employ when befuddled.

I suppose I was a split second away from either being knocked out or shot (or both) when my red-faced hostess ran toward us screaming.

"Wait, wait, wait, I know him, I know him! Let me handle it!"

The agents let her slip between them, and she calmly asked me what the problem might be. I explained my surprise gift for the President and showed her the jar and label. She said that was a "real sweet" thing to do, which I thought was a pun thing to say about honey so I laughed a little. I then strutted out of the White House, vindicated, proud, and clueless.

ABOUT THE AUTHOR

Frank Kilgore graduated from Clinch Valley College (now the University of Virginia's College at Wise), where he designed and completed the nation's first Appalachian Studies college major. He was the descendant of a dozen or so patriots who fought at the Battle of King's Mountain, and the son, grandson, nephew, and cousin of dozens of coal miners.

Frank was a country trial lawyer for nearly forty years, as well as an Appalachian conservationist, historian, and author. He helped establish the Appalachian School of Law and founded the Appalachian College of Pharmacy, both in Grundy, Virginia. As a dedicated defender and champion of his native Southwestern Virginia, Frank worked tirelessly to increase educational opportunities, preserve the area's spectacular beauty, and bring jobs and investments to the region.

Part of Frank's drive to bring tourism to the area included purchasing land in St. Paul, Virginia, for the popular Sugar Hill trail system, later developed as Clinch River State Park. All told, he designed and helped build over seventy miles of hiking and biking trails across what is known as Far Southwest Virginia, and mentored over a hundred at-risk young mountaineers along the way.

ALSO BY FRANK KILGORE

In addition to this book, Frank was the author of *The Clinch River: A World-class Treasure*, a science textbook highlighting the natural resources and conservation activities within the watershed. Soon thereafter he researched and edited *The Virginia Headwaters of the Big Sandy River: A Story of Revitalization and Nature's Resilience*, a textbook focusing on a neighboring watershed. Both books were donated to high school students as part of a place-based science studies project within their watersheds.

Frank's book *Far Southwest Virginia: A Postcard Journey*, co-authored with Katharine Shearer, came out in 2004. An expanded and redesigned edition titled *Far Southwest Virginia: A Postcard and Photographic Journey*, was published in 2014.

The starting point for *The History and Culture of Coalfields Southwest Virginia* was Frank's bestseller *J.D. Vance Is a Fake Hillbilly* from Fake Hillbilly Publishing, a full-throated rebuttal to Vance's *Hillbilly Elegy*. Frank's exploration of Appalachian culture and history from the point of view of a real mountaineer helped correct misinformation and inspire pride in a region too often overlooked or outright slandered by outsiders.

At the request of regional teachers and other educators, Frank started with much of the historic and cultural material of *J. D. Vance Is a Fake Hillbilly* and expanded upon it for *The History and Culture of Coalfields Southwest Virginia*, adding geology, natural history, and more emphasis on the accomplishments of our region's best and brightest.

Electronic copies of *The History and Culture of Coalfields Southwest Virginia* are available to regional high schools and colleges at no cost for use as part of their history curriculum.

www.ingramcontent.com/pod-product-compliance
Lightning Source LLC
Chambersburg PA
CBHW052135070526
44585CB00017B/1831